AF522349

Premchand
on
Culture and Education

(Translated from Hindi to English)

Premchand
on
Culture and Education

(Translated from Hindi to English)

Edited by
Shuby Abidi

AAKAR

Premchand on Culture and Education

Edited by Shuby Abidi

First Published 2020
Reprinted 2022

ISBN 978-93-5002-677-9

Published by
AAKAR BOOKS
28 E Pocket IV, Mayur Vihar Phase I
Delhi 110 091 India
aakarbooks@gmail.com

Laser Typeset at
Arpit Printographers, Delhi

Printed at
Sapra Brothers, Noida.

Contents

Translators

Ameena Kazi Ansari, Professor, Department of English, Jamia Millia Islamia

Keerti Ramachandra, translator and freelance editor

Madiha Masarrat, theatre practitioner, ex-student of the Department of English, Jamia Millia Islamia

Mohammad Asim Siddiqui, Professor, Department of English, Aligarh Muslim University

Poonam Sharma, MPhil in Modern South Asian Studies from Wolfson College, University of Cambridge

Ruchi Nagpal, Research Scholar, Department of English, Jamia Millia Islamia

Sami Rafiq, Professor, Department of English, Aligarh Muslim University

Shabeeh Rahat, Assistant Professor, School of Law, Delhi Metropolitan Education, Affiliated to Guru Gobind Singh Indraprastha University

Shaheen Saba, Research Scholar, Department of English, Jamia Millia Islamia

Shuby Abidi, Assistant Professor, Department of English, Jamia Millia Islamia

Urvashi Sabu, Assistant Professor, PGDAV College, University of Delhi

Acknowledgements

Editing a book is an arduous task, but it is more rewarding than I had ever imagined it to be. I wish to thank UGC-SAP-DRS-III for providing me the opportunity to take up this volume of *Premchand on Culture and Education*. I am indebted to Prof. Ameena Kazi Ansari, Coordinator, UGC-SAP-DRS-III and Prof. Anuradha Ghosh, Deputy Coordinator, UGC-SAP-DRS-III for all the support and guidance.

The translation workshops organized by UGC-SAP-DRS were instrumental in vetting the translations. I am indebted to Prof. Anisur Rahman, Senior Advisor, Rekhta Foundation and formerly Professor, Department of English, Jamia Millia Islamia, Prof. Asim Siddiqui, Department of English, Aligarh Muslim University, Kirti Ramachandra, renowned translator and freelance editor, Prof. Sudha Rai, formerly Professor, Department of English, University of Rajasthan, Jaipur, Prof. Mini Nanda, Department of English, University of Rajasthan, Jaipur who were visiting fellows to the UGC-SAP-DRS-III, Department of English and resource persons in various workshops.

I am grateful to Prof. Nishat Zaidi, Head, Department of English, Jamia Millia Islamia, for her constant encouragement and suggestions. Thanks are due to Prof. Anisur Rahman and Prof. S.Z.H. Abidi for their valuable suggestions and insights.

Many thanks to all the translators from Jamia Millia Islamia and other universities who have contributed to this book. The volume would not have been possible without their consistent participation, hard work, and patience.

I thank Tanushri Banerjee, Research Scholar, Department of English, Jamia Millia Islamia and Hanzala Mojibi, Student BA English (Hons.) for providing me with all the technical assistance required in drafting and editing the book.

My apologies if there are any inadvertent errors and oversights. I look forward to the earliest opportunity for correction.

Introduction

There are only a few exceptional writers who enjoy a steadfast popularity in both the Hindi and English literary world. Premchand is among those few. Applauded in the Hindi literary world as the Father of Modern Hindi fiction and bestowed with the title of *Kalam ka Sipahi,* Premchand's literary worth has exponentially shot up in the English literary scenario because of the availability of his creative output in English translation. Nearly all the established translators and literary mavericks have tried translating Premchand into English. To the extent that Premchand's whole corpus has now been translated into English. Premchand can be called a myriad minded genius who expressed himself in more than one artistic mode. Like many great writers such as D.H. Lawrence and Sri Aurobindo, he used multiple genres to express his central thoughts. He is undoubtedly a master of the genre of novels, short stories, plays and journalistic articles. He championed the genre of the novel and established himself as the undisputed 'Upanyas Samrat,' though, he gradually moved away from it and announced his significant shift to the genre of the short story. Stating the reason for this rupture, Vineet Gill quotes Premchand in his article "Hidden Gifts": "Novels are read by those who have money; only those who have money have the time, some are written for those who have neither money nor the time." (Para 9) Premchand was a versatile writer whose choice of genres was determined by larger social, political, and cultural circumstances. He said in *Upanyas*: "When social conditions are inimical to general prosperity, every choice a writer makes has to be justified in a political context." (Para 7) Choosing the genre of non-fiction/journalistic articles was an intelligent and appropriate decision. It can be conclusively said that no other genre suited the political, social, and cultural environment of the 1930s in India than non-fiction.

The 1930s was a turbulent, politically and socially charged decade. Mahatma Gandhi had waged war against the British. In his letter to the Viceroy, Gandhiji writes: "I had gone down on my knees to beg for bread, and what I have got instead is stone. The only language that the English understand is the language of force. The whole of India is one vast prison. I refuse to acknowledge this (British) law and consider it my sacred duty to shatter the scorching monotony of this compulsory and coercive peace which is stifling the nation......"(254) A staunch Gandhian that he was, Premchand decided to buttress Mahatma Gandhi's fight by paralleling it with his own Mahabharata, the one that he decided to fight with his pen. He decided to bring out *Hans*, which was followed by *Jagran*. The publication of these two journals witnessed the rise and popularity of non-fiction/essays and articles. They became significant fora for Premchand to voice his opinions, which he could not otherwise express. Emphasizing the importance of *Hans* and *Jagran*, Amrit Rai says in the biography *Premchand: His Life and Times*: "All three pieces ....had been published in one or the other of his own journals, *Hans* and *Jagran*. However, what he enjoyed writing best in his journals week after week and month after month were notes and comments on a wide range of current affairs of which he had ever been a keen observer. In this privilege lay the reward, a hard-earned one, of being the editor and publisher of two papers."(189)

Premchand's non-fiction carries the quintessence of his ideology. No genre other than non-fiction could have provided him the scope and complete freedom to execute, what he believed, was the ideal conception of a writer and literature. He indulged in direct and conscious didacticism in his articles/essays and editorials and wrote with a crusading zeal to uplift and educate the people. The expository nature of his non-fiction honed the perceptiveness of the masses to discriminate between the good and the bad. He provided them the much needed critical lens to analyse and critique life. Purposive and missionary non-fiction of Premchand enabled a peaceful social revolution and envisioned a utopian society based on truth, justice, and freedom. He forged a unique type of consciousness raising non-fiction to suit his commitment to literature as enunciated in his celebrated lecture "Sahitya ka Uddeshya".

Besides being a celebrated novelist and short story writer, Premchand was also a columnist in the journal *Zamana* with a portion entitled "The March of the Times." The very title of the section elucidates his predilection for the rising tides in society. Antagonistic to ivory-tower writing, he felt the impact of the events and evinced his interest and daily involvement in the current issues and events. The upheavals of the decade of the 1930s have direct or indirect documentation in the essays/articles/columns in *Hans* and *Jagran*, aptly earning the pride of being called a rich source for the historian and a repository of responses. The essays/articles have a remarkable topical relevance, along with being wide-ranging in thematic choices. Expressing his penchant for articles on current affairs, Premchand wrote: "So long as one is not in touch with current affairs one does not feel inspired to write an article on any subject and is hard put to find a subject anyway."(81) The articles/ essays are multifaceted and have newness of ideas. His awareness, observations, reflections, and experiences are embodied in them. Premchand's articles enjoyed mass appeal and popularity, and a significant reason behind it is his objectivity, which he achieved by denying active participation in politics or activism of any kind. He believed in literary activism and fearless expression of his mind. It was his intrepidity and credibility that added to the charm and novelty of his articles. Highlighting his indomitable spirit, Amrit Rai quotes Premchand:

> Both the public as well as the government wish to consider the writer to be their stooge. If the writer wrote as others wished him to, he could not be a writer and retain his individuality. His is a difficult task. If he offends the government, they put him in jail; if he offends the public, they threaten him with violence. Should the writer then give up writing? No, he should not. Whatever he writes is out of the deep anguish from within. Pity is that these people's minds are closed and they have entrenched themselves everywhere. But I am not at all worried about these threats. If I were, I won't be writing. If a writer were to worry about such threats, how can he give a lead to the people? (344)

Premchand viewed his profession of writing as a service to the nation. His journals, columns, short stories and novels smack of his patriotism, and immense love for India. He considered himself to be "a writer with a message, a writer with moral obligation to rid his society of many evils which he specifically pinpointed"(109) in his non-fiction. In the Presidential Address of the Progressive Writers' movement in 1936, Premchand had said: "I cannot conceive of literature as a soporific. If it is no better than a soporific, it is better than useless or dead. We must see to it that our literature possesses these fundamental qualities: dignified thought, the breath of freedom, beauty, and clarity of style, and a clear reflection of life's calm and bustle, the heart of truth. It must give us a goal, and it must make us alive, it must make us think."(22) Directly or indirectly, he wrote to awaken, enlighten, and educate the people. When he talks of a strong and united India, he does not always refer to the political developments or the freedom from the British domination. His reference is to the pillars of a nation—its culture, education, the future of India—its youth.

Premchand oscillated between his profession of writing and that of teaching. He was a school teacher and later served as Inspector of Schools for many years. His association with schools and students gave him a unique insight into the world of education and its relevance in society. His cumulative wisdom related to the world of education could not effectively spill over in his short stories and novels. His articles and essays, therefore, provided Premchand an essential platform to express his views and bring about a visible change in the educational system in India. The postulation of reformative measures in schools in his articles in Urdu journals *Adib* and *Zamana* fetched him the job of Inspector of Schools. Premchand pressed his pursuit by contributing articles to *Hans* and *Jagran* in the 1930s as well. It is not without concrete reasons that Premchand is counted among the top educationists of India along with Chanakya, Dayananda Saraswati, Dr. Sarvapalli Radhakrishnan, Swami Vivekananda, Savitribai Phule, and Rabindranath Tagore. Premchand believed in leading by example. In his long career of teaching, he practised later what he preached in his articles/essays. Corroborating this view, Amrit Rai says: "...His lectures were a source of all kinds of fascinating information. He spent his energy not in dictating notes to his students nor in drawing all kinds of maps and figures on the blackboard but in trying to make his students sound in body and mind..."(115) In his article "Shiksha ka Naya Adarsh," Premchand attacks the ideals of education as they make a person selfish, self-serving, snobbish, and insensitive. Lamenting the fact that our education system fails to awaken our social consciousness, he suggests competitiveness to be replaced by supportiveness and mutual trust. He gives primacy to childhood as an adult personality is shaped in it. Premchand emphasized formal education, but he never favoured the imposition of classes and strict discipline. His article "Sir P.C. Rai ka Deekshant Bhashan" reiterates a similar view. According to P.C. Rai, classes should not be made mandatory for students since the compulsion of acquisition of knowledge robs it of its beauty. He further denounces classes and examinations as they limit the self-development of students. Declaring them redundant, he cites the case of well known people who never went to schools. In another article, "Fail Hone Wale Ladke," Premchand opposes the examination system and failing of students in it. He believes that if colleges do not ensure jobs, then they have no right to impose such restrictions on them. To a great extent, he ascribes a student's failure to the personality and motivation of teachers. He believes in holistic education, which prioritizes extra-curricular activities like yoga, sports, dance, and music. Academic institutions of excellence like Shantiniketan and Madanpillai University are an exemplum. In the article "Dakshin ka Shantiniketan," Premchand talks about the growth of the university after Mr. Udh and Cajuns dedicated themselves to the university and used innovative and holistic techniques to impart education. In an article written in 1935, "Swaasth and Shiksha," he considers a lack of health awareness in the curriculum to be the biggest flaw of the modern education system. Premchand suggests teaching books like *Ways of Good Health,* which was taught to him in middle school. The solution to the defects of the modern education system can be found in the ancient teaching system called the Gurukul system of education. Articles like "Gurukul Kangdi me Teen Din" showcase the merits of the Gurukul system of education and plays up its role in producing more "servants of the nation than any other institution of learning." Recent researches in the field of education validate the relevance of the Gurukul system of education and emphasize the need to revive this ancient education system. It works on the fundamental concept of education from within and believes in character-building, which leads to nation-building. Premchand anticipated the New Education system way back in the 1930s. His radical views on education and vehement advocacy of reforms in schools and universities point towards his ardent love for liberty, national values, and freedom: it was his firm conviction that only fearless, honest, and strong men could lead to nation-building.

Premchand was a nationalist and nurtured the dream of a Swaraj. It was the driving force of his writings. Being an apostle of the Gandhian ideology, he knew fully well that freedom could not be attained unless Indians free themselves from the fetters of parochialism, discrimination and tread the ethical path of honesty, justness, and unity. It was self-evident that he was fighting twin battles—one with the British and the other with his own people. It led to a convergence of political freedom with the social revolution.

Premchand feared the jeopardy of the Indian freedom struggle by the devious British. Through his non-fiction and pamphlets, he exposed the selfish intentions of the rulers to thwart the desire for independence. The communal franchise in India is the raw nerve. He cautioned the Indians against it and created an educative environment. Articles like 'Tyoharon Mein Dange' and 'Sampradayikta aur Sanskriti' were written to combat the divisive policies of the British. Blurring the boundaries of the Hindu-Muslim divide, he pointed out that "now there is no such thing as 'pure' Muslim culture or Hindu culture, nor is there any other 'pure' culture. There now exists only one culture in the world and that is the culture of economics." He bridges the widening gulf by enunciating many cultural and sartorial similarities between the two communities. He 'exposes this call of culture to be mere pretence and sheer hypocrisy' and makes a plea to put an end to such blind faith and hypocrisy. The British had not only colonized a country but had also managed to colonize the psyche of its denizens. Deep-rooted cultural inferiority deluded the Indian minds to this extent that Indians firmly believed that all that is Western is superior and powerful, and everything Indian wrong and imperfect. Premchand attacks the colonized mindset in his article "Maansik Paradheenta" and analyses the Indian "mentality to blindly ape Western culture". Overawed by everything English, Indians are used to expressing themselves in English. Speaking in English becomes a parameter to judge individual capability. Premchand dissuades his countrymen from exhibiting psychological submissiveness and inspires them to take pride in Indian culture, traditions, customs, and attire. Western solutions to the Indian problem will only lead to destruction. Ingrained slave mentality and inferiority can not be erased easily by one or two articles. He hammered the ideas in the minds of his readers by producing more articles on similar issues such as "Rashtriya Karyon me Ghulami" and "Angrezi Bhasha ka Rog".

Premchand's unwavering love for his country, his burning sense of nationalism, and his concern for its culture and traditions turned him into a 'social pathologist' and a cultural custodian. The British targeted the Indian culture to sustain their presence in India. Painful realization of this fact made him tirelessly write to protect the essence of one's country—its culture. He accentuates the significance of Indian culture in the article "Maansik Paradheenta" and says: "What is the most valuable part of any nation or caste? It is language, civilization, thought, and culture." He further adds that the loss of culture will only lead to our destruction. Renewal of respect for one's culture and tradition was the only way out from dissipating the embedded sense of inferiority. Along with showcasing Indian culture as a bundle of positives, the demerits of Western culture were highlighted to speed up the awareness. One after the other, he wrote "Maansik Paradheenta" in January 1931, "Naveen aur Prachin" in November 1931, "Jagriti I," and "Jagriti II" both in September 1932 to counsel the brainwashed Indians. He very deftly compares the ancient Indian culture with the prevalent culture, which is, sadly though, a Western import. He accuses the West in the article "Naveen aur Prachin" and says, "Western culture has turned us mean ....Self-centredness is the most noxious lesson taught by the West ...after trampling the world's interest, it has now emerged as a phantom of greed." The Indian culture is presented as spiritual, non-violent, and selfless, and Western culture its reverse. He posits in Jagriti 1,"...in each element of Indian life is the existence of non-violence and religion. Struggle and war are essential to gaining control of and consuming the riches of the world. Non–violence gives birth to sacrifice and renunciation." Culture is that entire complex which includes knowledge, belief, art, law, morals, customs and any other capabilities and habits acquired by man as a member of society. Therefore, Premchand, as a cultural custodian, wrote on diverse issues that contributed to culture-formation or influenced the thought-processes of Indians. He expressed his views on cinema in *Hans* and *Jagran* on various occasions since he believed that cinema was a powerful and effective medium that impacted the youth. In the article "Cinema aur Yuvak," he discusses the adverse effects of violent movies on the youth. He denounces violent movies but votes for educational movies as they will make learning exciting and innovative. His bitter experiences in Bombay in the world of cinema made him realize that the improvement of cinema is only possible if it goes into the hands of "educated, enlightened, and people of character." Along with visual arts, he comments on ancient Indian art in this article "Bhartiya Kala ki Atma". Premchand reports Sir Malcolm Talley's deliberation at the Lucknow School of Arts where he is critical of the depiction of gods, goddesses and religion in ancient Indian art and appreciates the contemporary art being in sync with the contemporary milieu. He firmly believes that the soul of India is the soul of the Indian artist and therefore it should be free from the religious and communal bonds of expression.

Premchand was made aware of the transformative power of pamphlets, journalistic writings/non-fiction when he read the pamphlet on child widow remarriage, and subsequently decided to marry a child widow himself. He wrote his articles/non-fiction with the same transformative zeal. In order to make his articles authentic and a reliable document, he wrote them after extensive research and fact findings. His erudition and awareness informed his non-fiction. Like an efficient journalist, he builds his case point by point. The groundwork that went into his articles made it conspicuous and worthwhile to read. Praising Premchand's probing, Naravane says in his book *Premchand: His Life and Work*: "His essay on Primary Education in UP published as early as 1909 shows how deeply he had studied the effects of commercialization and education. The thoughtful essay can be classed with some of Tagore's famous lectures on education."(204) In the article "Sanyukt Praant me Shiksha ka Prachaar," Premchand used empirical data from the education census of 1931 and gave a gendered and religious perspective to discuss the growth of education among men and women. Likewise, in "Carmichael Library ki Heerak Jayanti" he has documented minute details of the library like the exact number of books and members. Along with it, he elaborates on the relevance and the essence of a sound library.

The relevance of a writer is gauged from his universality and popularity. Premchand's short stories and novels cut across boundaries in terms of acceptance. His non-fiction is equally acclaimed and reputed today after years of neglect. The issues in his articles have a bearing on the contemporary society. Recently, Rahul Gandhi quoted from his article "Sampradayikta aur Sanskriti" to refer to the communal situation raging in society. Premchand's non-fiction is often quoted and serves as an essential point of reference because it does not just talk about problems but also provides solutions that are congruous with the recent problems. The positive and the negative are clearly defined and demarcated, which render it timeless. The conflict between the British and the Indians gains a universal dimension as it becomes a metaphorical tiff between good and evil. The countermeasures provided by him in his articles on culture and education are all measures for nation-building, which are relevant even today. Premchand was always ahead of his times, be it fiction or non-fiction. He gave equal status to non-fiction and 'prose of thought'. Lamenting the death of the novel, V.S. Naipaul some time ago posited non-fiction as the genre of the future. In his times Premchand saw the potentiality of non-fiction and gave us a rich corpus not just as a gloss on his novels and short stories but as a *sui generis* genre emerging from his profession and his milieu. He was indeed an avant-garde writer.

A writer's world view is constructed from his whole and complete oeuvre. Premchand's world view was formed by his short stories and novels and not his non-fiction. It is, therefore, not surprising that Premchand's non-fiction/journalistic writings/essays have been sadly and grossly neglected. Equal treatment has not been meted out to his genre of non-fiction. Consequently, one can easily figure out a glaring paucity of criticism and research on his non-fiction. A spate of books and criticism exploring innumerable facets of his short stories and novels have been repeatedly attempted and beaten to death. Researchers have hardly focused on Premchand's plethora of non-fiction. This volume and the other ones on his non-fiction will hopefully fill this yawning gap and enable students as well as common readers to have access to the English translations of his non-fiction and renew their interest in this forgotten and long neglected genre of Premchand.

Shuby Abidi

1

Three Days at Gurukul Kangdi (*Gurukul Kangdi Mein Teen Din*)

Madhuri: April 1928
Translator: Urvashi Sabu

The last *Aashadh*[1] I got an opportunity to visit Gurukul Kangdi. I had wanted to do so for a long time but had never mustered the courage. What would an irreligious man like me do at this centre of Vedas and vedaangas? As luck would have it, the Sahitya Parishad decided to hold its annual function at the Gurukul and invited me. I jumped at the opportunity. It was the fulfilment of my heart's desire. I left from Lucknow at night and arrived at Haridwar early the next morning. Two *Brahmacharis*[2] were there to receive me at the station. I had a taste of the Gurukul's principles at the station itself. A *tonga* was booked. The *tongawala,* thinking we were new to the place, asked for eight rupees to go to Kankhal. The *Brahmacharis* quoted six. The *tongawala* perhaps stuck to eight. The *Brahmacharis* had already quoted the reasonable fare. They found it below their dignity to exchange words with him. They walked

---

1. It is the month of the Hindu calendar that corresponds to June/ July in the Gregorian calendar. In Vedic jyotish, Asadh begins with the sun's entry into Gemini.
2. People who follow the concept of Brahmacharya which means "conduct consistent with Brahman".

half a mile and booked another *tonga* for six rupees. The first *tongawala* agreed to six, begged forgiveness for his crime, was prepared to accept his mistake, but the *Brahmacharis* knew no pity. He had tried to cheat the travellers, and he had to be suitably punished; in the eyes of justice, pity has no value.

The *tonga* reached Kankhal in half an hour. We alighted and reached the *ghat*. The hills in front of us stood resplendent in green. The Ganga below came springing, gurgling from the lap of the mountains. There are many streams here, which unite in the rains and flow further down from Kangdi. I thought we would cross the river on a boat, but there was no sign of one. The current here is so rapid, the river bed so rocky that no boat can get far. People use rafts to cross the river. This is a kind of rough boat where tin canisters are used instead of terracotta pots. Many canisters are placed lengthwise and tied securely with bamboos and ropes. The raft is broad from the middle and narrow at the ends. A first-timer will have serious doubts about the ability of this contraption to get across the river. However, this suspicion is put to rest just a few minutes into the journey. This raft cannot sink. No matter how rapid the current, how horrifying the whirlpools and eddies, how speedy the wind, how high the waves, this tiny boat will not be vanquished. If a man sits carefully on this boat, he can travel to eternity, but not sink. This insignificant little thing valiantly facing the raging river seemed like a lone soul marching against all the odds towards eternal light.

Barely half an hour into the journey, it began to pour. Our clothes were drenched, and a strong wind began to blow. The waves were not just jumping; they were positively pouncing. The raft frequently struck the stones on the river bed, and we almost fell into the churning waters. We reached Kangdi at around ten o'clock.

II

'Much ado about nothing'; this was the spontaneous thought that occurred to me when I first set eyes on the buildings at the Gurukul. There is only one structure that can be called a building, but even a high school building would be in better condition than this one. Three years ago, there were many buildings on this campus; but the floods of 1924 destroyed many of them, and the verdant garden was inundated with alluvial soil. The ruins of the fallen buildings can still be seen. We were accommodated in a tiny house, called the *pucca* Dharamshala. Respected Pandit Padmasinghji Sharma[1] had also arrived. We both stayed in this room. Just as we had finished bathing, lunch was served. We sat down to the meal. The *pedaas* were delicious. Hospitality is the specialty of this institution. Its food will satisfy even the most insatiable appetite. I was especially delighted to see the *Brahmacharis*. Such simple, dedicated young men are not to be found in our English medium colleges. The pedantic atmosphere so rife in the Sanskrit colleges of Kashi was conspicuous by its absence here. Here, the guest of the school is the guest of each student. He will lay your bed for you, fetch water, and will help fold dhotis too. This school appears to be more of an ashram than an educational institution. I've never seen such enthusiastic young men. Whatever they do, they do with complete dedication. They have no laziness or indolence and are always eager to know and learn.

The Sahitya Parishad function took place in the evening. The Acharayaji delivered his talk. The *Brahmacharis* read out their papers. Some were literary, and a few were

---

1. Famous author and critic from the Dwivedi Age. He was a Sanskrit scholar with a great command on Urdu, Persian, Marathi and Hindi. He died in 1932.

historical. It would be amiss to judge these papers on very lofty literary parameters. These were not the writings of seasoned intellectuals, but they would make any school student proud. The music was disappointing, though. There is no music education in the school. Perhaps music is considered a hindrance to celibacy. However, I could not see any religious bigotry here. I was pleasantly surprised by their freedom of ideas. I could not find a trace of political, social, or religious narrow mindedness in their ideas.

There was a dinner get together the next day. Students and teachers alike sat on floor mats and ate. Here in our English medium colleges, we sit on chairs and tables for our meals. This anglicization seems not to have even touched this place. Our communal rituals, customs, and ideas can be preserved and protected only in such institutions. Maybe preserving them is no longer a priority these days. Today, only he is a pure Aryan who, in all other matters, is a slave of foreigners, but will not hesitate to abuse followers of other religions.

There was a poetry reading event in the evening today, chaired by Pandit Padmasinghji. The *Brahmacharis* read their compositions. Most of the poems were laughable, but I appreciate their courage for their complete lack of hesitation in reciting their crude attempts at poetry. This youthful courage is commendable to some extent. I have seen students who suffer from terrible stage fright. This audacity is better than that hesitation. However, it is better to not recite such poems before an audience, which will make it laugh in amusement. After the poetry recital, Sharmaji delivered a thought-provoking lecture and regaled the students. He is as generous and straightforward as he is learned, and hospitality is his forte.

On the third day, we dined at the house of the Chief

Patron. I still have not forgotten the taste of that delicious meal. Ramdevji is amongst the few who are gifted with such eloquence that one can listen to him and be regaled for hours. He is well versed in English literature and an expert in Indian history. The *Brahmacharis* have absolute devotion to him. The Gurukul may not accomplish much, but the ideal of simple living and high thinking, which it upholds for its students, is reason enough for it to keep alive. English medium colleges teach us to be slaves of our necessities, and teachers are the biggest propagators of this art. What progress will those young men make in life who are shackled by the chains of necessity? They may get good government jobs, but government jobs do not make a nation. The Gurukul has produced more servants of the nation than any other institution of learning. Valid service of the nation lies not in getting high degrees and posts, but in taking responsibility for the uplift of the nation. Of the 141 graduates of the Gurukul so far, 87 have entered public life; it would not be wrong to say that the encouragement that Hindi has received from the Gurukul is unmatched by any other institution of learning. Whatever doubts existed about the usefulness of the Gurukul have been dispelled by seeing the public life of its graduates. Of the 141 graduates, twenty-nine work in other gurukuls and nine are in the literary profession. Twenty-three are preachers for the Arya Samaj, 5 are successful healers, 18 are in business, and seven have gone abroad for further studies. Two have returned after passing the exams; Dr. Prannath has recently returned from England after having become a doctor and another gentleman has become a barrister. Last year, four *Brahmacharis* appeared for the Senior Cambridge examinations, and three passed. This makes it clear that the *Brahmcharis* are given ample practice in English too.

Mr. Satyavrat Sidhatalankar[1] has recently written a book on *Brahmacharya* in English, the style and language of which are beyond reproach. It is a matter of great pride for any university student to write such a book.

The Gurukul campus also houses a school of Ayurveda, where students are taught about various herbs, roots, and fluids. They are also imparted knowledge of anatomy and biology. We hope that Ayurveda will be in competent hands with the healers trained at the Gurukul. They are no quacks, they know the elements of the human body well, and are also knowledgeable in surgery.

No words can describe the natural beauty of the Gurukul. Strong characters can only be built in such surroundings. The Ganga flows playfully in front of the Gurukul; the hills sing silently behind. To the left and right extend miles upon miles of rosewood and catechu trees; breathing such clean, filtered, wholesome air is itself an exercise in self-purification. The *Brahmacharis* swim long distances in the lap of mother Ganga. Where in the polluted air of the cities will one find such qualities? Nevertheless, the last flood caused such damage to the buildings of the Gurukul, that it has now become necessary to change its location. Arrangements are being made for the same.

---

1. Satyavrat Sidhatalankar was a reputed educationist and Parliamentarian. He served as the Vice-Chancellor of the Gurukul Kangdi Vishwavidyalaya. He has authored several books on the Upanishads, Homeopathy and Yoga.

2

Make the Children Independent
(*Bachchon Ko Swadhin Banao*)

April 1930
Translator: Shuby Abidi

Many will be surprised by the very title. Boys are innately independent. Right from infancy, they refuse to be bridled and tamed. So the moment they become somewhat sensible, they run uncontrolled. The need of the hour is that they should be taught obedience, respect for elders, and patience. Teaching them independence would be like adding fuel to the fire.

Children today are more independent than what their parents used to be at this age. It is not surprising if the consequences of this tendency of independence make the parents slightly sceptical; therefore, it is all the more critical that they are educated to be independent. The more potent a child is, the more independent he will be, but we do not train them into it. If young men have to be admitted to the armed forces, they need to be taught drilling. If they want to be a singer, then it is impossible that they start singing without any professional training even though our children are more independent now than they were in the past. We are not giving them the proper education to solve this problem. In short, children should be given an education which can protect them in their lives.

It is an established fact that children of today are independent, and nobody can change this state of affairs. There are various reasons for it—the exodus of families from villages to cities and settling where they are free from the pressure of family and acquaintances, weakening of old customs and traditions which had a significant influence on the rebellious youth. Newspapers, motor cars, and cinema strengthen the proclivity of independence.

There is no point in shedding tears over this. In the old days, when there was this rule of respecting and obeying the elders, and each low caste bowed before the higher caste people, then children were taught to respect right from childhood and rightfully so. However, when we are teaching them to obey the orders of external powers, then we are turning a blind eye to our children's most significant need. In the circumstances that youth face today, respect and humility are not as important as personal beliefs and professional freedom.

What is the intention of this new type of education? Obedience is and will always remain an integral part of our life. If everyone does what they please, then the moral fabric of our society will get shattered. In fact, these essential elements should be protected in every household, but at the same time, their parents should try not to make their children feel that they are some stone idol or riddle. Wise parents should try to make their behaviour as natural as possible because the objective of children's life is not to obey orders but to enter professions. In reality, when boys receive this kind of education, they lose self-confidence. They always wait to take orders, believe no one would like to give this kind of education where they develop such habits.

The second rule is that parents should not decide

everything but should leave it to the boys. Once a king, while handing over his son to a teacher, advised that he should make himself dispensable as soon as possible. It is not our duty to make our boys obey us all our lives; instead, we should make them capable enough that they can decide which direction they want to take in their lives. The appropriateness of education is relative to the degree of this tendency of independence in youth.

The third rule is that households should also run on the patterns of democracy. We know this from experience that no matter how much we believe in democracy but in our homes, autocracy rules. Like Mussolini or Kaiser, the head of the family takes them wherever he wants. Sometimes it is just the opposite. No law or rule prevails. They do whatever they want, and no one bothers about the other. Boys, young men, and older men go their ways. Both ways are miles away from democracy—the first rule lacks freedom, the other sense of responsibility. Both these rules are unsuitable from the perspective of the education of youth. What should be done is that right from the beginning, even in home affairs, children's opinions should also be taken. Even a small child starts understanding his responsibility if he is put on the right path. Children love and respect even those parents, who misbehave with them. But parents crush this tendency, and we see the terrible consequences of this nearly every day.

Even a common man is proud and happy to know that he has a special place in the house and that he is an integral part of it. Even a child does not lack this feeling. The biggest secret of a successful family is that they should bring into use this behaviour. Such children will always protect the dignity of their families. Here he is getting the lesson of forming an independent opinion. Some people may have a bitter experience about this, and young men would have cared only for themselves and not paid attention to the welfare of the family. In their opinion, vanity and indulgence are present in today's youth in higher proportion but, it is not the fault of the child but that of parents. We need time, patience, intelligence, and sympathy to educate our children. It means that the moment children understand the difference between income and money, they should be given money in their hands and should be trained by giving fixed pocket money, and in adolescence itself, they should be trained to value money and learn to spend it within the limits of income.

We do not pay attention to these things. Many parents are as indifferent about their children as they are about their pet dogs and parrots. If we take a test of the family circumstances of the wicked and noble children, it can be proved that the weaknesses that enter a child's character are because of the carelessness of their parents.

If we have to inculcate freedom in children, then they must be allowed to do some work. Usually, it is understood that the duty of good parents is to keep their children away from all difficulties. As a result, children from affluent families become lazy. When they get everything without doing anything, why should they do any work? Interestingly, a broad principle of philosophy is that children enjoy nothing as much as doing something on their own, building something on their own. A boy feels happier in putting his paper boat in water than he is to see his large ships sailing.

In our established institutions, now people have realized that making the children do some work is a first grade mental and moral worship. It should happen in every household. There is no better way to develop self-confidence in boys.

In wealthy families, it is considered demeaning to do something with their hands. There are servants for children's work. There are motor cars for going out. They are given neat and clean clothes to wear for going out and are instructed that they should not soil them. There are movies and cinema halls to entertain them where they have to use their eyes to see; they do not have to do anything. This habit of dependence that they develop does not desert them for their entire lives. Such children brought up in luxury, are the ones who harm their brothers in their selfishness and unnecessarily flatter the government.

We often get anxious to see the boys doing some new work. He is touching the clock, Oh! He might break it. Here he touches the pen, and there the parents raise a hue and cry; this should not happen. Children's natural creativity should be awakened. If the child wants to make toys, wants to fish, grow vegetables, stitch clothes, wants to blow a trumpet, act in plays and write poems, do not stop him. If a child stays even a few weeks in natural surroundings, steers boats in rivers, drives the motor car in the field, works with a spade in a farm, then he will experience and gain tremeadous self-confidence which he might not be able to get from books or preaching. It is surprising that those who have spent their lives in difficulty save their children from work that enhances the excitement of life-struggles.

We want to share here what we mean by self-dependence? It does not mean we do unchecked whatever we please and whatever we do not. It means that instead of external pressure, there should be the dawn of self-control in us. A truly independent man is one who, whose life is disciplined by the rule of mind, who does not need any external pressure. Children should have enough judgment as it enables them to figure out the merits and demerits of every action with the help of their inner sight.

3

Mental Slavery (*Maansik Paradheenta*)

January 1931
Translator: Shuby Abidi

We want to rid ourselves of bodily dependence but are voluntarily increasingly getting trapped in psychological dependence. What is the most valuable part of any nation or caste? It is language, civilization, thought, and culture. This culture is what makes a Hindu a Hindu, a Muslim a Muslim, and a Christian a Christian. Towards the preservation of this culture, Muslims stay away from the Hindus fearing that mingling might corrupt their culture. Likewise, Hindus also want to protect their culture, but whether Hindus and whether Muslims, while clamouring for the protection of their culture they are hell-bent upon destroying it.

Culture (civilization or refinement) is a comprehensive word. Our religious views, sociological conditioning, our political principles, our language and literature, our lifestyle, and our behaviour are all a part of our culture. Finding the West all-powerful, we are trapped in the illusion that we are entirely wrong, and they are perfect. Owing to this blind devotion, their demerits appear to be merits and our virtues our flaws. Let us take the example of language. Today English has become the preferred language of our cultured society. Official language that it is, we have to use English in the offices; but we have become such an ardent devotee of the power of this language that we have come to rely on it even in our personal letters and intimate conversations. The wife writes to her husband in English, the son writes to his father in English. When two friends meet, they converse in English. If any assembly is organized, it is in English. Even a diary is written in English. What a language! What accommodativeness! So poignant, what power for expression of thoughts, such a vast vocabulary. Its literature is so precious and sophisticated. Its poetry is so poignant and prose so meaningful. Everybody is fascinated with English. To the extent that it has become the parameter to judge our capability and scholarship—whether we are adept in writing and speaking English. From Class 8 onwards, English idioms are memorized, discussions carried out on minute differences amongst synonyms. They stake everything in delivering British speech with the right accent and pronunciation. If the British are unable to pronounce a word because of some oral make-up, we try to generate the same flaw in us. There are very few amongst us who can pronounce such a common word like "the", the way the British do. This mentality of ours keeps growing with our national sentiments. To the extent that English alone has become the language of the educated class. Whenever one or two English words get expressed in our language, we do not apologize for it. It is sad that even those who are not well versed in English flaunt their knowledge in English itself. An English person would never even in his dreams speak in any other language to another Englishman. However, here in India just by speaking in English, we portray our mental slavery. I cannot even imagine the mentality which inspires speakers who share a common language to use English. It makes some sense if you use English while conversing with a Bengali, South Indian, or Chinese. It is essential to talk to them, and as of now, there is no Indian language which all Indians know. Why should people, from one region speaking the same language, speak in English? Why should they write letters in English? Why should they use "morning-morning" instead of saying *pranaam* or *namaskaar* or *vande* or *Namaste?* Why should we only use "Hello"? I cannot even imagine! There is no paucity of people who take pride over borrowed roles. They must be happy with the thought that people think that they are the owners of this language. Probably this is the mentality that operates among the English users. Either they mean to prove who speaks better English or they want to make it clear that the British cannot speak English with the clarity which we can. As a result, one learns to speak and write good English, but one forgets one's mother tongue considering it to be contemptible. It, more than shameful, is the tragic mental slavery of our educated class.

French poets compose poetry in French; the Germans write in German, a Russian writes in Russian. At least regarding those creations they take pride in, they are written in their own language. However, in our country, all the poets and writers would start writing in English lest they get a publisher. Those who get a publisher do not miss the opportunity, no matter how much they are scoffed at by the English critics. They are contented.

We agree that the English language is very mature; it can express all types of emotions. It is not yet so with Indian languages. However, when the same people who are creators and custodians of their mother tongue become devotees of the English language, then the future of one's own language will be diminished. Will you then build the walls of Indian nationality on the foundations of foreign literatures? This is sheer stupidity. Today our educated class has severed itself from the masses. Their lifestyle, speech and attire separate them from the masses. Probably their joy knows no boundaries thinking they are unique. Maybe they consider the masses to be inferior and rustic but, actually, they are the ones who have fallen in the eyes of the public. They do not influence the masses; instead, they are condemned by calling them "spoilt", "sahib bahadur". God forbid, if they are even seen being beaten by the British, they will make fun of their miserable state, and no one would even go near them. Just look at the slavery, that in our schools even Urdu and Hindi are taught through English. If the pitiable Hindi Professor does not use English as a medium to teach Hindi, then the students consider him to be incompetent. If one is disgraced, one will be embarrassed and will try to hide it, at least one would not be proud of it. Instead, we parade the disgrace of our slavery; even feel proud of it, as if it is a medal of our reputation and banner of our fame. Bravo Indian slavery, I am delighted!

Let us leave language and talk about clothing and attire. Can you see that gentleman in a cap looking hither and thither? He is our Indian European. Step away; *Sahib Bahadur* is coming. Salute *Sahib Bahadur*, you are *sahib bahadur* in totality. However, you seem to be a slave, from head to toe, who shamelessly exhibits his slavery the same way that a prostitute exhibits her style. You definitely have spiritual strength, self-esteem of great magnitude. You reject popular opinion and do not bother about others' opinions and selfishly do what pleases you or strictly do what you feel is good for you. Why respect popular opinion? No slave to popular opinion, just tell this statue of self-esteem to go to an English club without wearing the felt cap, he will be nervous, his blood will curdle, and his face will turn pale. Why? Because his self-esteem is only to intimidate one's countrymen, there is no essence in it. They cannot neglect even the minor conventions of this society where they want to belong. They do not bother about the public because they could not care less about whether they are angry or happy. They become extremely servile in the presence of those who can harm them in any way. I once asked my *Saheb Bahadur* friend: why are you so stylishly dressed? He replied with great conviction—"We dress this way because we have to meet the English and we do not have to remove our shoes." Those who wear traditional Indian clothes, like *Achkan*[1] and *Topi*[2], have to remove their shoes. I believe that those who meet the British with some work have to take off their shoes because their soul is indebted and those who go without any work even if they wear traditional ethnic wear like *mirzai*[3] and *achkan* need not take their shoes off. However, the state of such people is like the man who, in order to hide one single spot, colours the white cloth black. If your self-interest makes you helpless, it is better to remove one's shoes rather than commit the sin of shamelessness. Don't think the British respect you because of your coat and pants. Moreover, even if it so, seeking respect by surrendering your identity and dress, is like accepting a bowl of curry by selling your national pride. I questioned another friend of mine to which he replied—it is very comfortable while travelling, people take us for some influential person, and they do not barge into our compartment. Another gentleman said: "English clothes make us feel very fit and active." People will offer

1. It is a knee length jacket worn by men in the Indian subcontinent.
2. A light weight helmet worn for protection from the sun.
3. Mirzai or bandi is a type of jacket in black and white worn by men in Madhya Pradesh.

different arguments of this sort to resolve the problem. I ask: Why gentlemen, are fitness and vigor to be found only in English clothes? Is it something magical that the moment you wear it a current of strength will run through your body. These arguments are weak. Yes, but there is some validity in this argument that when the whole world is trying to emulate European attire, then how can we be different? Alternatively, a second argument can be that we do not have one regional, national dress. Better to have one European outfit than different types of regional dresses. Undoubtedly it is a tricky question. This issue deserves our attention; all the other countries have one dress for both rich and poor, with the difference being only in the quality of cloth material. In our country the farmers wear *mirzai* or *kurta dhoti*, a few wear *shalwaar*[1], a few *pagdi* or *janghia*[2]. First, have the luxury of one racial framework then only can you object to the Western attire. Like language, uniform attire for the whole nation has just manifested. This cannot be created through an institution or policy. India will have to wait for long for a worldwide dress. However, till that time comes, in my opinion, we should keep this policy in mind and respect popular sentiments. If in any region, the public wears coats then coats and pants can be considered to be suitable. Likewise, in regions where the masses wear *kurtas*[3] and *dhotis*[4], then in those areas, *kurtas* and *dhotis* should be respected as the regional dress. It implies that the educated class, just to prove their uniqueness and dominance, should not use attire that reflects foreignness. It is quite possible

1. Worn with a kameez is a combination dress worn by women and in some regions by men in South Asia.
2. Vernacular term for underwear.
3. Upper part of a type of long shirt worn with pajamas.
4. Loose cloth wrapped around the waist like a wrap-around. It is a traditional informal wear in North India but a traditional formal dress in South India.

that a few people do not feel proud even after wearing Western clothes, and with no intention to realize a selfish objective. Unfortunately, western dress is not appreciated by the public and one who wears such an apparel, may even be a god, is perceived to be a rebel, and a disciple of the ruling country. It may become our national dress after we gain independence. Though much neglected now, then it would not be considered irreverent. Just think, does it behove educated people that they mould their lifestyle so that people should fear and hate them rather than respect them? Frequently rejecting public opinion can have adverse results, and it is obvious, that if public opinion had supremacy, then the anglophiles would think twice before wearing English outfits. However, had this outlook been limited to the issues of language and dress only, then it would not be a cause for anxiety. However, this attitude has dominated our other social perspectives and today if we do not put an end to it, then our national culture will disappear. It is quite natural that the subjugated race will notice only negative things in themselves, whereas the ruling race will be nothing less than a bundle of positives. Our culture teaches us that we should not increase our needs so that we can help and benefit family and community. Western culture is based on this principle, stretching your needs as much as you can, even if you have to cut down your expenses. Live for yourself and die for yourself. Our culture is basically agrarian; we stay in villages, where mingling with near and dear ones keep us away from all ills. Western culture is business-oriented and is involved in creating new cities, where we sever all ties and get involved in misconduct. In our culture, the joint family was an integral part. In Western society, the family only means man and wife. Both have merits and demerits, but in one servility and sacrifice predominates, in the other one selfishness and narrow-mindedness. In our culture, courtesy has great importance. In Western culture, self-praise has the same status. Praise yourself and blow one's own trumpet. In our culture, the position of money is not relevant; respect is attained through knowledge and behaviour. In Western civilization, money is the most important thing. We also earn money but along with sympathy. The Westerners also earn money, but there is no trace of sympathy. The basis of our culture is morality, and the basis of Western culture is battle.

However, we are not here to praise our virtues. What I intend to say is that our mentality to blindly ape Western culture is a result of our mental defeat. Our culture also has defects, but blind devotion to European civilization is not the remedy. We should have found the solution from our own culture. By blindly aping the Western culture we will perforce have to use the same solutions. Europe has lost the right path and is unaware of its objectives. European intellectuals also state today that European culture is moving towards its destruction. Should we also prepare for the same destruction? Just understand, this political situation will not remain, but in the present circumstances we have lost our identity. We have lost the power of morality, and if we lose our culture, then we will be destroyed.

4

Slavery in the National Pursuits (*Raashtriya Kaaryon Mein Gulami*)

April 1931
Translator: Ruchi Nagpal

It saddens us deeply that English still holds the same position in national pursuits, and whatever Mahatmaji[1] had said to Congress activists, about the Hindi language, has not been paid heed. If people from other provinces take shelter in the English language in our province, then it can be forgiven, but the problem is that the Congress activists of this province take pride in writing letters in English, publishing reports in English, and circulating notices in English. If the national language is being affronted at the hands of national leaders, then whom should we complain to? Maybe reading and writing in the national language appears like contradicting their ideals to them. They want to impress the audience with their command over the English language. If this is their mentality, and could not be anything else, then such gentlemen are pitiable because they are merely beating the drum of their psychological

1. Mahatma Gandhi emphasized the use of Hindi as the national language. In an interview, Mahatma Gandhi said, "I do not object to your learning English for the sake of acquiring knowledge or for the sake of earning your livelihood but I object to your giving so much importance to English and giving a low place to your national language, Hindi."

submissiveness. Many of them are highly qualified in English. They must be wondering if they are to read and write in Hindi then why should they learn English. It is also possible that they do not have a passion for writing in Hindi. If this is the case, then the readers must boycott such people. What Congress does in other countries for propagation, that being in English is acceptable to us. We have to look up to English for provisional correspondence for a few days. However, it is shameful to take recourse in English and is equally against the national ideals to use English for the matters which are confined to this province. At least those from this province who cannot write Hindi script as fluently as they can English, should be ashamed of themselves.

5

The Disease of the English Language (*Angrezi Bhasha Ka Rog*)

September 1931
Translator: Shuby Abidi

We have already drawn the attention of the readers of *Hans* to this issue. It really pains me to write that even our national workers are as much a victim of this disease as the government servants, lawyers, and college teachers. There is no doubt that they have started wearing *khaddar*, but there is not even an iota of culture and tradition to be found in their mentality. Go to any committee meeting, and you will find the khaddar- clad gentlemen conversing in fluent English. The words and sentences, which they have read in papers or English dailies, which are eager to flaunt do appear the moment they get the opportunity. It is hilarious when this gentleman shows his elegance of speech in English in the presence of women who do not even know English. How long will this spell of English last and linger over our heads? How long will we remain a slave to this language? It only proves that our nationalism has not reached the depth of our hearts. We do not see any leader except Mahatma Gandhi propagating the Hindi language. It should be clear that as long as our national language is not nurtured, the development of our nation will remain an idea and a dream. A Japanese expresses himself in Japanese, a Chinese in Chinese. An Iranian in Persian but an educated Indian takes pride in studying and speaking English. Many gentlemen do not hesitate to say that they find writing and speaking in Hindi difficult. This is a simple slave mentality. Even the most distinguished Indian speaks in English when he talks to a White man. Not once does he think why an Englishman cannot speak in Hindi? Well, talking in English with the English can still be condoned, but there is no justification for conversing in English amongst ourselves.

6

Military College's Organization (*Fauji College ki Aayojna*)

September 1931
Translator: Ruchi Nagpal

In order to Indianize the military in India, we need military officers, and for the training of the officers, a college should exist. A committee was formed to formulate the scheme for the foundation of one such college, chairman of which were the military lords. The committee has published its report. I was dismayed at the sight of it. *Laat* Sahibs[1] want to qualify 60 officers from that school every year. Non-official personnel of the committee take the count to one hundred and twenty. India has 4,000 military officers. According to this, if they decided not to admit any English officer, it would take 35 years to train these officers. Furthermore, according to the number given by the *Laat* Sahibs, it will take 70 years. It only proves that the government desires to increase the tenure of its military hegemony. When the war was going on in Europe, youngsters were trained for a few weeks and were sent off to the war; and they performed their duties with great skill. At least there was no complaint against them. However, in India, it takes 35 to 70 years to train 4,000 officers. This fairly manifests the intentions of the

1. It was a sarcastic way of referring to the senior officials during British colonial rule.

government. If I may ask, why do we require 4,000 officers? When the safety of the nation would be our responsibility, we will decide whether we need more officers than this or less. For the same expenditure, we can open two schools and the task which was to be completed in 35 years will be finished in 17 years. In my opinion, there is no need to have a separate military college. Like we have provision for Science in our schools; similarly, we can make provision for military education. To extract a mouse after digging a mountain is our government's old policy. Nevertheless, we are glad that after many commissions and committees, this situation at least has arisen. Now we have to see how much time it will take to put this report into action. The report says that the college will be opened in 1932. Let us see.

7

The Ancient and Modern
(*Navin aur Prachin*)

November 1931
Translator: Shaheen Saba

There was not much difference between ancient Eastern and Western cultures. Since a large chunk of new tradition was a Western import, it has been called so. The Western culture managed to bedazzle us for a long time. So smitten were we by the glitz and glamour that we looked down on what was beautiful and simple in our own. Look at the restrictions regarding time. Our tradition was such that a friend or acquaintance could walk in unannounced. We were happy conversing with them. Neither were we ever troubled by such visits, nor did it appear a waste of time. In our eyes, providing solace to a friend is more valuable than money. However, now, we weigh everything on the scale of money; hence the visit of someone who is of no use to us seems poisonous. Spending even a minute on a well-wisher who drops into pour his heart out or for a little laugh, seems burdensome *now.* Because nowadays time is money. Humanity, compassion, and consolation have no use. Money is all that matters.

Nowadays, the entry and exit labels figure on the gates of the affluent. Enter for those who are of use and exit for those who serve no purpose. And we are not tired of praising this culture. By throttling humaneness, the Western man has become an emotionless machine. That is what it is teaching us. The Eastern tradition swelled with happiness with the visits of guests; they consider a guest to be the harbinger of good fortune regardless of whether they came in the middle of the night or the previous night, there is no lack of hospitality. They are provided the best space in the house, served the best meal, and the entire household is at their service.

Western culture has turned us mean. A guest arrives, our soul almost flutters away. How as such a calamity descended on us? Now we try to persuade him to leave as soon as possible. The head of the family pulls a long face, and his wife's brows are furrowed. It appears as if something inauspicious has cast its dark shadow over them. *Babusahib*[1] cannot leave his room. The guests are settled in the verandah. The mistress of the house is not a slave to cook and serve anyone who walks in. Preparing meals for the family itself is a difficult task. Where did this messenger of death come from? Moreover, look at the daring; they did not even inform the host in advance; some excuse could have been made, being unwell or going out. When the guest departs, it is as if a new day is born. We have turned so selfish, so mean that we rarely do anything without our self-interest in view. If he has brought a court case, or if there is a chance of ensuring a seriously ill patient or there is a possibility of getting a big order through him, everything changes. The guest is looked after so well as if the whole household's life depends on his well being. Here too, the same craving for money, the same anguish. As for these gentlemen, the more they are soaked in these colours, the more parochial they become.

1. Here Premchand uses the term ironically for people who have no time for others and consider themselves very modern and educated.

This attitude is not so evident in the villagers, labourers, and traders compared to the educated, civilized society. To serve themselves is the sole objective of their life. I do not contend with attributing new with evil and the old with good virtues. In traditional hospitality, some irresponsible worthless guests make a nuisance of themselves. However, being hospitable to them had an element of decency and generosity, but this new narrow mindedness is pure selfishness and self-centredness.

Self-centredness is the most noxious lesson taught by the West. After trampling the world's interest, it has now emerged as the phantom of greed. It is heartless without any tenderness or pain. Selfishness fills people from head to toe and from within to outside. Neither laughing and talking nor crying or singing is free of selfishness. In ancient tradition, it was improper for a doctor to charge a patient. He needed to visit a patient's house, irrespective of the hour. The doctor often gave the medicines himself or prescribed them; he never imagined recovering his fees from medicines. Serving patients was his duty. The doctors took pride in this. However, we can see what has happened today. What remains is a partial duty. Many *vaidhyas* or doctors do not charge fees from patients at home, but they manage to earn something through medicine. This is the self-fashioning that the West has given us in these hundred and fifty years. There were lawyers and teachers in old times, too; lawyers received their wages from the government, and teachers survived on alms for imparting knowledge. Today, humans have turned into idols of selfishness. Even if we have talented humans today, they will not be beneficent to the world. They will amass properties, visit mountains, spend on drinks, and be on cloud nine. Why should service be free? The western guru has taught him this new lesson. Nowadays, even *Mahatmas* do not give blessings without money. Earlier, the success of intelligence and knowledge lay on the mantra of servitude, now in self-fulfilment. A doctor cannot leave without fees even if a patient is breathing his last. This is an opportunity to charge double or four times the fee. Does one get such a catch every day?

When we have devotees of selfishness all around, the well has been contaminated, how can we accuse our poor teacher? They will also go to Europe and draw a massive salary upon return. Building a career is life's motif! Salute the West! Your ways are stranger than God. Will those old days return where tradition was not stained by poverty? Is there hope?

8

Two Convocations of the United Province
(*Sanyukt Prant ke Do Convocation*)

December 1931
Translator: Shaheen Saba

India does not have a university. Yes, there are factories for producing graduates. In this case, the United Province[1] is the Lancashire or Bombay of India. There are five such majestic factories here where the youth is taught to waste life, turn spendthrift, luxury-oriented, and inculcate false pride. BA pass means that the concerned youth is distinguished in all the evils mentioned. He has nothing to do in the office except pushing his pen. The poor folk are not at fault. He has been manufactured in this machine. After all, whatever he has witnessed, heard, and read appear before him. Visit any university. You will not have a trace of Indian ethics anywhere. It is dominated by language, dressing, and manners that are English. The principles of sacrifice and love have been lost. Here, only those with the highest degrees from England are scholars. The contribution of

1. The United Province was a province of British India which came into existence on January 3, 1921, as a result of the renaming of the United Province of Agra and Oudh. It corresponds approximately to the combined regions of present-day Indian states of Uttar Pradesh and Uttarakhand.

these educational institutions in creating a 'fashionable' community is exceptional. One who has stayed within its premises is under its spell all his life. The per capita income of an Indian is three rupees per month at the most, but our accomplished youth cannot survive on less than sixty rupees. He consumes the portion of twenty people on his own, but their teachers consume the share of at least two hundred people. Such is the plight of a poor country like India, where the government officials are paid many more times than those in the rich countries of the world. The same darkness envelops our educational institutions because it is also a part of the same administrative machinery. Our Vice-Chancellor wants a salary of Rs. 3,000 per month. When the chief head of the educational institution is setting such an example before the students, it should not appear surprising that the students also turn out to be money hoarders. It will be justified on the grounds of the professor's pay in England; however, England and India cannot be compared.

Nevertheless, Sir Raman lectured at the convocation at Allahabad's factory and Sir Radhakrishnan at the Lucknow factory. Sir Raman is an accomplished scientist and Sir Radhakrishnan, a distinguished philosopher, but there was a massive difference in their addresses. Sir Raman praised Prayag and called it an ideal educational institution. However, when the question of subsidy was raised in the factory, the factory organizing committee decided to increase the students' hostel fees, because there was no question of decreasing the teachers' salaries. This is the condition of the unit upon which our *Swaraj* is based. Sir Raman also did not hesitate to compare Prayag University with Harvard. This is very unfortunate that the universities where our students' futures are shaped are steeped in selfishness. We do not bear grudge against other departments. Their existence rests on power politics. They extract as much as they want and spend in whichever way they like. We are helpless. However, universities are the ideal seats of our civilization. Sir Raman said that—"We are the custodians of a great civilization,"—but the way selfishness has overpowered us has left us upset for our future. We expect that the universities should spend less at this time of financial crisis. Then only will the other government departments see sense. At least we could save our faces and be proud of our educational institutions. However, adhering to such a policy has proven that they are not less selfish than other departments. Our educational institutions followed some other principles, and they can be seen in a smaller version in the Gurukul system. The most astounding thing that Sir Raman said was—

"It is not the duty of colleges in Hindustan to intensify the speed of revolution; their duty lies in acting as brakes to the evil of the caste system." Sir Raman could not understand the gravity of the current Indian revolution. The Indian revolution is the desire to win over one's soul. We can see that Europe's independence, artificiality, and heartlessness is gradually gripping India. Our colleges were set up with this view, and the government has been successful in its enterprise. Our revolution is an attempt to reclaim our lost spirit, sacrifice, simplicity, and principles. It is directed towards removing this Western aggression and selfishness and desires, whereas ours is to see cooperation and harmony. Braking this speed indicates that we must quietly witness the downfall of India. One must extinguish the fire as soon as it breaks out in the house because a delay could mean disaster.

The fearless and nationalist lecture of Sir Ramakrishnan at Lucknow University is an exception. Without caring about the whims of the officers, he fearlessly spoke the truth. The role of the colleges/educational institutions in a revolutionary period and expectations from the students were placed before the audience like a true patriot. We have always heard that philosophers care for nothing except beating around the bush. There are many comic stories prevalent around the philosopher, but by delivering this speech, Sir Radhakrishnan proved that a philosopher could also be sad at the country's sad state and understand the duty of the educated lot at this hour. We have never heard such an inspiring and profound lecture at any convocation. Each line of that lecture was heart warming. He said:

> An intelligent person does not contend that he can express some opinion on every subject; neither does he summarize a writer in a sentence nor satirize the principles of civilization. An intelligent person can view liberty, originality, and other human emotions in a far-sighted manner. He has compassion for the difference in opinions.

Further, he focused on the older principles of schools as follows:

> In ancient days, the values of colleges were compared to a lightened torch that passed from one hand to another and from one generation to another. This torch is mighty. It has raised many revolutions, stirred commotion. It is the carrier of the spirit of revolution; it is the fire which clears by burning the weed and dirt. If the social, economic, and political fire emanating from these revolutions scares us, we must stay away from educational institutions.

He added further that the students in the colleges must be high spirited. If educational institutions produce such humans who are stone-hearted, scared for their lives, slaves to luxuries, who do not wish to take any risk, then such institutions cannot fulfil their duty. If it turns enthusiastic and courageous youth into heartless, selfish human beings enslaved to traditions and if the emotions are frozen, then they have moved far from its duty.

This address is so inspiring and didactic from the beginning till the end that one must read it repeatedly.

9

Swami Shradhanand and the Indian Education Committee (*Swami Shradhanand aur Bharatiya Shiksha Pranali*)

January-February 1932
Translator: Ruchi Nagpal

Swami Shradhanand[1] was a pioneer of ancient Aryan ideals, but according to me, the work he has done for the resurgence of national education is unparalleled. In the times where education has become a marketable commodity, it was Swamiji who saw the element of nation-building in the ancient Gurukul tradition. The kind of education children receive shapes them as individuals. Our schools are the most prominent keepers of our culture. Education institutes should be wholly independent whether the nation is independent or dependent. Any kind of help from the state is equal to the entanglement of education. Moreover, if there is a chain restricting the education system, then it is no surprise that the students whose interests are fostered by such an education will have the attitude of a

1. Swami Shraddhanand (February 22, 1856-December 23, 1926), also known as Mahatma Munshi Ram Virji was an Indian educationist and an Arya Samaj missionary who propagated the teachings of Dayananda Saraswati. This included the establishment of educational institutions, like the Gurukul Kangri University.

slave. State ideals get changed, but the ideals of the nation remain the same. If the ideals of the nation change, then its great tradition will be crushed, and it will lose its identity. Gurukul tradition lived through the Buddhist era. In the Muslim era, this tradition was confounded, and the nation-state came undone. There was no control on any domain of life, whatsoever. Letters and hermitage, which were the pillars of the Aryan tradition, lost their real face and stemmed into caste and class and saffron-robed, lethargic, and corrupt individuals took the place of hermits. Under the English rule, new schools came up, but their ideals and their goals were different. It was only a department of the bureaucratic rule whose purpose was not the search for truth or the advancement of civilization but to create a row of workers for the bureaucratic rule. The books and the teaching methodology all had imprints of British rule. The self-respect of students was crushed there. It was a business enterprise which always tried to extract something from the students at every step. There was a long list of fines. If one was absent, the fine was due; if one was late then one had to pay the fine; any mischief and the fine must be paid, lesson not learned and fine becomes imperative; and then there is a fee for everything—school fee, library fee, science fee, examination fee, stationary fee. Hoping that students from such educational institutes will serve the nation is sheer bleakness. Their soul has been crushed.

Compare the ancient ideals of our nation with these Western ideals. Our Vice-Chancellors draw a salary of Rs. 3,000 per month. How fabulous is your mansion, and how wonderful are your wheels, what a lifestyle! The Principal also draws around Rs. 2,000. You do not have a mansion as fabulous as Vice-Chancellors but you prefer expensive cigars. You have an approach to women and are fond of horse riding. Professor, reader, lecturer, dean, tutor, demonstrator, all have the same power, pomp, and splendour. What is the question of character in such an environment? A hermit will also succumb to the Western fashion and riches, and therefore there is no questioning our tender-hearted young men. By looking at the obligingly falsifiable competitions in the world, our youngsters delve into the same attitude. Cigar and lavender, numerous suits, and God knows what else torments him and stimulates his imagination. In order to fulfil these temptations, he lies, provides excuses, and uses trickery. He even loses his dignity and self-respect. He becomes unable to face the hardships of life. He seeks shelter from someone or the other. He cannot stand independently. One who gets bewildered if not given tea on time, and gets crazy if not given his cigar for a while; how will such an individual face the struggles of life? Even such situations produce gems, once in a while. However, this is an exception.

Raise your eyes towards the ideals of the past. Chancellor is the high idol of education, a storehouse of knowledge, who has tasted the odds of life, and is beyond the temptations of the world. Teachers, similarly moulded in such ideals are without any pride and show. In ancient ideals, the pride is not in who is more spendthrift, or who has the best dogs or who goes to the cinema more often but rather who is more self-sufficient, who has more devotion and excellence, who has the attitude of service and cooperation. There is a stark difference between the two ideals.

Swami Shradhanand resurrected this national ideal. Time was not in his favour. There is no need to mention the people against him, hardship after hardship. But he was as courageous as he was idealistic. Without caring about anything, he laid the foundation of gurukuls. Albeit, society had some influence on gurukuls as well. Graduates coming out of gurukuls stepped into a different world, wherein they had to change some of their beliefs in order to live a respectable life. That model, vivid and beautiful, glowing with the ancient traditions, looking at the fake and false principles not with condemnation but with pity, is standing tense with the different situations— in the hope of good days.

10

The Days of Talkies are Numbered (*Swaak Filmon ke Din Gine Huye Hain*)

August 29, 1932
Translator: Ruchi Nagpal

It appears that the hype of talkies would soon be gone. Silent[1] movies used to get popular everywhere within a year. Australia, China, and Russia, everywhere people could seek joy in Charlie Chaplin's jocularity. Talkies'[2] is a restricted domain. Only those who know the English language well can enjoy English cinema. The populace of a country is never so eloquent in a foreign language to understand it and derive pleasure out of it, and therefore producers of talkies are trudging a steep hill, and this condition will not pertain for so long; silent cinema will return, it is hoped.

1. Silent films were the films that had no synchronized soundtrack.
2. A film with soundtrack as distinct from a silent film. It is widely referred to the movies with soundtrack and audio during a time when mostly films were silent.

11

Awakening 1

(*Jagriti 1*)

September 1932

Translator: Mohammad Asim Siddiqui

Sleep is as important for life as waking. Both states depend on each other. Inability to fall asleep is a disease which creates problems of many kinds. And the creature who sleeps day in day out is like a dead being. If both activities complement each other, a human being awakes to do work and sleeps to rest, life becomes comfortable. But waking is life's main symptom, sleep or rest only helps it. That is why waking is a sign of life and birth and sleep of decline and death. Waking is a passion-dominant activity. Sleep has the dominant element of inertia. Many techniques and remedies have been suggested for not sleeping much. Nobody has suggested a technique for sleeping a lot in the same way as many efforts are made to keep healthy but nobody has made an effort to fall sick. Indeed the absence of health is an ailment in much the same way as the absence of light is darkness. The less a person sleeps the more aware he is, so much so that some scholars are of the opinion that sleep is not an essential activity. Maybe sleep is not important for ascetics whose being consists of *raj* and *tap*, having been freed of *tam*[1], but for ordinary creatures also the rule of

1. One of the trigunas (sattva, raja and tama)

not sleeping more than required applies. Therefore when we desire an awakening for a nation then it seems that that nation has become too inert and it does not have the required signs of life. We are in that state and are trying to get out of it. We know that we badly need awakening. But we have some disagreement about what should be the nature of this awakening, this rise. Different thinkers talk about different principles. We plan to discuss this subject in the first few issues of *Jagran*.

First of all we should be clear about the aim of our life. Unless we are sure of this, we cannot have a stable picture of awakening. Just as human beings differ from each other and what is nectar for one, is lethal poison for the other in the same way nations differ. There may be different reasons for this—natural condition of a country, different climate and different traditions. If we do not make these circumstances our guide and make our path favourable to these circumstances, it is possible that instead of achieving our goal, we gradually move away from it. We will have to follow our civilization which is here since eternity because civilization is the substitute of these circumstances. In other words, whatever is the nature of civilization; it is the result of these circumstances. When we think about that civilization, we realize that it is predominantly duty, religion, God, non-violence, renunciation and principles-oriented civilization. It has the principle of that harmony between man and nature that they, instead of being enemies, complement each other. Man has the freedom to earn riches and valour, but their use should be in the interest of society and the nation, and not for cheap consumption, and domination over weak people. 'Non-violence is the greatest religion' and 'the world is one family' are the essential elements of our civilization and we follow them even in this condition. Although for many reasons that civilization has become defaced; countless negative things have entered there so much so that its form cannot be recognized, still in unfavourable conditions these two elements exist like pillars of light. Despite losing a lot whatever remains in our civilization is the gift from these two pillars of light, otherwise our boat would have sunk in the whirlpool long ago. From this we reach the conclusion that the aim of our life is not power but earning of the highest good. The aim of our life is not the blind worship of selfishness or the accumulation of the riches of the world in our kitty but to live in the world in a manner that nobody comes to any harm from us, nobody's life comes to a risk because of us. Our ideal characters are not like Napoleon who wanted to dominate the world or like Clive, Cromwell, Lenin and Mussolini. Our ideal characters are kings like Krishna and Ram, warriors like Arjun and Bhishma and a family man like Gandhi. We believe in cooperation and not conflict.

It is said that all civilizations are similar in principle. There is no difference between the East and the West. Non-violence, love and service which are the essential elements of our civilization are also the basis of Western civilization. Whatever difference there is, is in the new and old civilizations. The old civilization of the West was identical with ours. Selfishness and conflict had a dominant presence in the West ever since the beginning of the machine age. Although it is not a good thing to say that Greece and Rome, which mark the zenith of Western civilization, were conflict-dominant nations. Christianity which is another form of Buddhism and Hinduism in many respects was like that plant in the West which had been implanted from outside. For a certain period it fought the hostile forces with its internal strength, and then it was destroyed. The foreign plant could not survive in a hostile climate. Today despite being called Christians, Western people are miles away from Christianity. Christianity's values of mercy and non-violence do not exist there. Rome is famous for its poets, philosophers and warriors but there is a doubt if there was a renouncing ascetic there. It was a consumption- dominant civilization and all sections of the country were eager to consume more and more the result of which was inevitably mutual conflict. In India we do not see this kind of conflict in ancient times. Maybe the reason behind this is that the powerful had suppressed the weak so much that the latter did not have any spirit left in them. Or the spirit of sacrifice and service was so pronounced that there was no room for conflict. We have the tales of the fight between the angels and the devils but that was the fight for principles and not self-interest. The devils were consumerist and the angels were sacrificing. The angels fought for self-defence and the thought of dominating the devils did not cross their minds. On the contrary there was the fight of self-interest in Europe. It was the fight of the rich and the poor, of the rulers and the ruled. The mark of that conflict is visible in all elements of Western civilization. Christianity suppressed that natural tendency for many centuries. In the end it was defeated. Consequently the madness of selfishness in European civilization is the natural result of that tendency. Repeated occurrences of revolution are the result of that selfish struggle.

We will discuss this question again next week.

12

Awakening 2
(*Jagriti 2*)

September 1932
Translator: Mohammad Asim Siddiqui

In the last issue we had discussed Europe's struggle and India's love of non-violence and love. The essence of our civilization is non-violence, and that of the West is struggle. Not that there is no existence of non-violence in the West or that it is unusual to see conflict in India, but we are not discussing exceptions here. Struggle inheres in every capillary and in each element in the West. In the same way in each element of Indian life is the existence of non-violence and religion. Struggle and war are essential to gain control of and consume the riches of the world. Non-violence gives birth to only sacrifice and renunciation. The victor from Europe tries to get maximum advantage after achieving victory in a war. Here Arjun sinks into shame and dispassion, Ashoka becomes a monk after reaching the pinnacle of dominance and makes his life meaningful by preaching religion. Conflict leads to polarization; for fear of one group swallowing the other group, each group organizes itself and tries constantly to defend its interests. There is no evidence of such groupism in India. No group feared the other group to such an extent that it needed to organize itself. Each group had a defined area of work. It used to lead life in that area. The Brahmin was the leader of society, not because he had the power of money, or muscle but because he had the power of education. The *Vaish* used to earn money but he used to spend that money on public interest. The tendencies were such that people cared more for their duties than rights. The king of that time did not simply impart glory to the throne; he rather cared for the interests of the people day in and day out. He used to spend some of his time daily to listen to people's woes and problems which begot in people a sense of devotion and respect towards him. The landlord did not content himself by merely collecting taxes from farmers but used to protect the interests of the people. It was his religion to ensure the digging of wells and ponds and giving his all during a calamity. There were surely greedy landlords, but they had a bad name in society and for this reason they did not dare to oppress the people.

On the contrary there is the reign of selfishness and greed in the West. The invention of machines has spread the air of consumerism. This consumerism is the bane of the Western civilization. The extent of harm that this consumerism has caused to the world and will cause in future too, is really without any parallel. It is the result of this that people who used to work from their homes are compelled to work like slaves in the mills. The mill owner wants to pay them minimum wages after getting maximum work. This struggle has become so widespread that in every country of Europe there is a vigorous effort to overthrow it. Russia has overthrown it but in other countries too there is this struggle, more or less. In the mills a few men can do the work of many people that is why several people remain unemployed. To help this unemployment, goods are produced excessively in mills and for the consumption of these goods markets are searched for. Consumerism and imperialism thus have a meeting ground.

13

Delhi's Jamia Millia: A Report
(*Dehli ke Jamia Millia ki Report*)

November 1932
Translator: Ameena Kazi Ansari

Delhi's Jamia Millia is one of the Muslim institutions which has truly placed the ideal of service before the nation. Earlier, Jamia (meaning 'university') was established in Aligarh through the efforts of the late Hakim Ajmal Khan Saheb. After the Non-Cooperation Movement of 1920, it received a setback as public enthusiasm waned, and it had to be shifted to Delhi. It functioned here, with assistance from some local organizations and princely states but mostly from the public. However, once the freedom movement began, donations from princely states dried up; there only remained the support from the public and the cooperation and sacrifice of its employees. Even in these circumstances, its teachers served with great devotion and enthusiasm, surviving on just a pittance. They were all so capable that they could find employment in any institution, but they chose not to abandon Jamia Millia and bore all kinds of hardships, continuing to serve Jamia with contentment and irrepressible enthusiasm. Despite all these difficulties, Jamia has a few of its own buildings, its library, and its publication division. Jamia has now obtained two hundred and fifty acres of land seven miles away from Delhi in

Okhla to construct more of its buildings. Such is the power of working with missionary zeal! Here, there is no sign of the Muslim tendency to seek favours from the government. Jamia is a living example of self-confidence, self-sufficiency, and patriotism.

14

Sir P.C. Rai's Advice to Youngsters (*Sir P.C. Rai ka Yuvakon ko Aadesh*)

November 1932
Translator: Ruchi Nagpal

In his lecture at Lahore University, Sir P.C. Rai[1] strongly condemned the amorous psychology of the youngsters, that by being a slave to their desires, they were doing great harm to themselves as well as to the nation. The words might have appeared somewhat harsh to the students, but if they think carefully, then they will realize that the path they are hurtling on is not suitable for them. Gone are the days when they were often welcomed after their education. The present situation is such that it might take them years to experience such an occasion, and it will still not arrive. Now only those youngsters will triumph who can keep their needs to a bare minimum. Till now, your parents have showered you with love, but a time will come when they will expect you to serve them and you will be burdened with household requirements.

If you remain a slave to your desires, then it will be very troublesome for you. We agree that these days are for

1. Prafulla Chandra Roy is one of the famous scientists that India has ever produced. Considered as one of the luminaries of the Bengal Renaissance, P.C. Roy was an eminent scientist, an exemplary entrepreneur, a patriot and a passionate teacher.

you to enjoy life, but you must also understand that this is the time to prepare yourself for future challenges. If you have developed the habit of thrift, if you do not hesitate to do your work, if you are not addicted to smoking, drinking, and drugs, then the field is yours. You will be happier with less, but the habit of being a spendthrift will definitely make your life problematic. You will be able to experience the true happiness of life. A matter of concern is that the ideals which are put forth by the universities do not encourage frugality. The students always look up to their teachers. The students try to imitate the intellectual vigour and behavioural aspects of their teachers, and our teachers dress in the best clothes to look inspiring. A look at their attire one is mesmerized as if there is a competition among them as to who is more fashionable. The teachers must be wondering why they have received such prestigious degrees if they were to have a frugal lifestyle? What was the purpose of going abroad and doing all the hard work that they did? They do not go out and ask people for anything. They earn and provide for their luxurious lifestyle themselves, and they have all the right to do so.

Nobody has the right to interfere in their personal life. Why should they not reap what they have sown? Only an ascetic will have any objection to such a thing. There is no other place for youngsters. Whimsically, they will come to the class, pay the fees and attend the lectures. There will be no discrepancy in the luxurious life of the teachers. What then, enjoy life and deliver the lectures. You can live happily without bothering about the impact of your up-to-the-minute lifestyle on students.

15

The New Vice-Chancellor of Allahabad University (*Allahabad University ke Naye Vice-Chancellor*)

November 1932
Translator: Urvashi Sabu

We believe the entire province will be delighted to have Shri Pandit Iqbal Narayan Gurtu unanimously elected Vice-Chancellor of Allahabad University. The voting was as expected. We residents of Kashi will be deprived of Panditji's expertise at that crucial moment when the very existence of Kashi municipality is in danger. In your short term here, you had established yourself as a determined personality, and it was hoped that had you continued for another year or two, the municipality would improve further. We are sorry to see you leave, but at the same time, happy that you are now going to work in an area to which you have dedicated your entire life, one which is in dire need of your advice. Our university programmes are now outdated. A university is not a graduate producing machine; neither is the taxpayers' money meant only for examination awards and teachers' salaries. The nation expects universities to maintain high ideals, where rote learning is within limits, and character-building is the goal.

16

Health Check Up in Schools
(*Schoolon Mein Swaasth Pareeksha*)

December 1932
Translator: Ruchi Nagpal

The trend of health check up is a routine task in our schools. Once every month, the doctor pays a whirlwind visit and examines all the boys from a class within 5 minutes. He gets done with the health check up of the entire school within half an hour. To some, he mentions tooth decay, to some an eye disease, and goes his way. Such inspections never benefit the boys and are mere tokenisms. Nowadays, parents of the students are called and the doctor gives them a small health report of their award and bids them well. The report of the event gets published in the newspapers the next day. It fulfils their desire. All this is mere propaganda; there is nothing fundamental in these schemes. In my opinion, a suitable person for this health check up is the one with whom students can share their problems without any hesitation. Training colleges where many subjects are taught must make health and physical education its priority. These progress and health reports are all futile and worthless. The main thing is the physical and mental health of the boys, and this brief monthly check up is a mere formality. This thing should be strictly focused upon, and only a teacher can do so.

17

Education Convention in Gorakhpur (*Gorakhpur Mein Shiksha Sammelan*)

January 1932
Translator: Ruchi Nagpal

In the non-gazetted education convention in Gorakhpur, Mr. D.N. Kapur delivered a very thoughtful speech from the position of the chairperson. By criticizing the current examination conduct, you said that in England, a similar education committee has recommended that the examinations should be minimized, and for the Primary Course, only English and Mathematics should be taught. According to the Committee, examinations in these two subjects will firmly determine the academic development of the students. The situation is such that all the strength of the students gets directed in examinations. Scouts, exercise, games, debates, clay modelling, etc., which lead to the creative and psychological development of students, get sacrificed at the altar of exams. The sole principle of students is to pass the exams, and that of teachers is to ensure that they are cleared. The rest is mere ornamentation. This mentality to examine has led to the ruin of the education system, and it is no exaggeration to state that this is the reason for the physical depletion of an educated society. Our teachers are still dancing to the old tunes. The impact which their narrow approach has on students, the way their foundation is getting weakened, how cursed is their anaemia; all this is imperceptible to the teachers even when it is clearly visible to them. Exams are conducted for the subjects which were selected for their entertainment and humour, which further increases the number of examinations. On the one hand, there is the English language, and on the other, there is the terror of examinations. The students are getting crushed between these two grinding stones. It is a matter of joy that the education committee has now been drawn to pay attention to these shortcomings and it is possible that there will be some improvement in education conduct, but our teachers are too dogmatic, and there is a doubt if they would be willing to proceed in this direction. The obsession with English is overpowering them. This same speech was delivered in English. Professor D.N. Mukerjee is Bengali, but his entire audience was not Bengali. He could have delivered his speech in Hindi, and if our teachers are not capable enough to express their views in the language of the masses, then they are not ethically bound to be teachers.

18

Editors' Conference (*Sampaadak Sammelan*)

February 1933
Translator: Ruchi Nagpal

On the coming 26th, 27th, and 28th of February, the editors' conference will be organized in Indore with famous editor honourable Mr. Indra Vidyavachspati as the chairperson of the event. All the work that has been done in this area appears meaningless to some extent. Conferences and talks happen, but nothing fruitful comes out of such events. The dismal condition of our writers, editors, and journalists today is rather hard to explain. Editors are mere pawns in the hands of publishers and newspaper agencies. Anyone can be thrown out of a job on a mere whim. An editor himself does not respect another editor; a writer takes pride in insulting another writer. Editors who are writing for a humiliating amount by way of compensation or those who toil day and night, running newspapers at a significant loss, both are in a pitiable condition. Now is an appropriate time for the editors' conference to address such issues.

19

Promotion of Education in Consolidated Provinces (*Sanyukt Praant me Shiksha ka Prachaar*)

May 1933
Translator: Ruchi Nagpal

Numbers related to education from the census, which was carried out in 1931, tell us that in 1911, the literacy rate was 34 per cent per mile. In 1921, it was 37 per cent per mile and in 1931, 47 per cent. If we consider the exact numbers, then there were 16,20,000 literates in 1911, 16,68,000 in 1921, and 22,60,000 in the year 1931.

If appeared from a gendered perspective then:

In 1911, literate men were 15,05,945 or 61 per cent per mile.

In 1911, literate women were 1,12,520 or 5 per cent per mile.

In 1921, literate men were 15,56,626 or 65 per cent per mile.

In 1921, literate women were 1,32,246 or 6 per cent per mile.

In 1931, literate men were 20,43,410 or 80 per cent per mile.

In 1931, literate women were 2,16,228 or 10 per cent per mile.

Although there is commendable progress in the last decade, when compared to other nations, it is still less.

The average literacy rate in different provinces is as follows:

Banaras— 192
Dehradun— 173
Gharwal— 173
Almorah— 167
Lucknow— 123
Baliya— 124
Nainital— 159
Janaul— 145
Agra— 143
Mathura— 140
Prayag— 118
Kanpur— 139
Jhansi— 137
Fatehpur— 118
Aligarh— 115
Meerut 109

From the perspective of women's education, Dehradun ranks first— 54. After that, chronologically come Lucknow, Agra, Banaras, Nainital, Allahabad, Meerut, Mathura, Farukhabad, Jhansi, and Bijnour.

These numbers tell us that the literacy rate of men is highest in Kashi and of women it is highest in Dehradun.

Now from a religious perspective:

	Men	*Women*	*Men*	*Women*
Religion	1921	1931	1921	1931
Arya	293	337	93	84

Hindu (Sanatan)	74	94	7	14
Jain	568	590	77	128
Sikh	327	375	56	37
Muslim	74	97	8	16
Christian	318	327	209	314

The literacy rate is highest in the Jain community after which comes the Arya Samaj and then Christians. Hindus and Muslims are at the lowest. In the context of women, Christian women are the most literate and then the Arya Samaj women. Hindu and Muslim women are inconsiderable in this context.

20

Shantiniketan of the South
(*Dakshin ka Shantiniketan*)

June 1933
Translator: Ruchi Nagpal

Shantiniketan[1] is considered up as an ideal education institute in north India due to the charity and hard work of poet Rabindranath. The institute has not acquired this status for no reason. Without any doubt, it is better governed and organized an institute than many of the government schools and colleges. Shantiniketan, Kashi Vidyapeeth[2], and Prem College are such independent education institutes in north India that we are proud of, but there is a paucity of such institutes in south India. It is a matter of delight that on the premises of Shantiniketan, an institute has started working in south India. Twenty years ago, famous educationist, Mr. Ernet Udh established 'Madanpillai University' in

1. Shantiniketan is in the neighbourhood of Bolpur city in Bolpur subdivision of Birbhum district in West Bengal, India, approximately 165 kilometres north of Kolkata. It was established by Maharshi Devendranath Tagore, and later expanded by his son Rabindranath Tagore whose vision became what is now a university town with the creation of the Visva-Bharati University.
2. Originally named Kashi Vidyapeeth, the university was renamed Mahatma Gandhi Kashi Vidyapeeth in 1995. Babu Shiv Prasad Gupta and Bhagwan Das established the university in Varanasi, on February 10, 1921, during the non-cooperation movement of the freedom struggle. It was inaugurated by Mahatma Gandhi.

Madanpillai. After that, he left for abroad. Meanwhile, the University continued imparting education on the basis of Madras University. However, now, Mr. Udh has returned to India. He, along with his wife, has decided to spend the rest of his life in the service of this University. Apart from him, famous academician, traveller, and resource person, D.J.H. Cajuns has decided to dedicate his mind, soul and wealth to this college. The work has started with new vigour. Education will be imparted through new techniques. The University will aim to promote the cultural spirit and impart holistic education. Music will be a compulsory subject for Classes 1-4. Games and physical training lie in the hands of an expert. Both subjects are compulsory. Those who take leave from the games and yoga class without submitting a medical certificate will be marked absent for the entire day.

The University is built on 60,000 square feet, and the campus covers an area of 75 acres. In the Madanpillai area, *Bahuda* River separates the University. There are many proper fields for sports. In the hostel, there is space for a hundred and ninety students. There is a separate hostel for girls.

The university campus will function from the coming month of July; the classes have resumed from the 14th of June. We acknowledge the efforts of this institute and wish Mr. Udh and Cajuns success.

21

The Boys Who Fail
(*Fail Hone waale Ladke*)

July 1933
Translator: Shabeeh Rahat

It is a strange joke that when a student fails during his school and college days, he is punished. He is rusticated from his institution, and after being mercilessly thrown out, why should any other institution admit such an expelled boy! This is how the doors of education close on him from all sides. Such a pitiable condition. However, another problem arises here; if these students are allowed to stay on, how will the newcomers get a seat? However, these students must also get an opportunity. The problem is that this thirty-three students' cap is absurd. Either we establish enough schools so that all students might study, or else the existing schools should be allowed to lift this cap and create more space. Or else, the best way would be to make examinations even more straightforward, in which the maximum number of students could pass. When the school or college degrees do not help in getting a job, then why put so many restrictions on the students? Is it then only the fault of the boy that he fails? Do the teachers of the school hold no responsibility towards this? Agreed, the teacher cannot spoon-feed, but it is undeniable that the success or failure of a student depends to a great extent on the personality, diligence, and motivation of the teacher. On what grounds then are the students who fail thrown out?

22

The Arrival of the Education Minister in Kashi (*Kashi Mein Shiksha Mantri ka Shubhaagman*)

August 1933
Translator: Ruchi Nagpal

With the advent of the Education Minister, there was much hustle and bustle in Kashi for two-three days. It seemed as if the Governor or Viceroy was coming to the place. Because it is only when such personalities visit that there are police forces lined up on the roads. Now it seems even ministers have been accorded such a high honour. It is to be seen what privileges will be extended with the new administrative policies under the Swaraj.

23

Lucknow University
(*Lucknow Vishwavidyala*)

August 1933
Translator: Shuby Abidi

This year Lucknow University increased the fees of its law students by Rs. 25. Many savings were incurred from the law classes, but it was not considered enough. In a way, the institution has acted sanely. There is no place for new lawyers in law. Something needs to be done to stop this inundation. In my opinion, better results would be visible if there was an increase of a hundred rupees. Students will manage Rs. 25 from somewhere. Everything is slow. Let something be fast. It is a very beneficial policy to accelerate or speed up education. Lucknow University should hike the fees twice. Their profits will rise to a great extent. Even the government is always thinking of hiking the prices rather than reducing the expenses. The university is only a part of that government.

24

Red Literature in Hindustan
(*Bhaarat Mein Laal Sahitya*[1])

August 1933
Translator: Ruchi Nagpal

The Indian government does not want red journals or red literature, to connote communist literature, which advocated armed revolution, to be precise, Russian radical literature to be popularized in our country. We also do not want the red revolution, but what is red literature, reading which makes us crazy is something we do not know. This is something that India's prominent book distributor Shri S.B. Taraporwala & Sons, also does not know. Therefore, he wrote a letter to the government and asked which books they consider 'red' so that he may disseminate the information among the masses through newspapers, but the answer which he received from the government clarifies that they cannot decide anything about the matter. They are hesitant to issue a policy. The government can give such an answer, but what should the Indian journalists and book distributors do? According to the new law, they can seek bail through a paper for the publication of a part of a book which was hitherto being read and circulated. They can

1. This exactly is the question that Premchand raises in the write-up. From the current context one could perhaps label the writings of Marxist thinkers as 'lal sahitya'.

consider that part of such a book provocative. The book distributor can also be considered a criminal for keeping provocative literature. This is a very hostile situation, for which the government must clarify its policy.

25

A New Plan of the Film World (*Film Sansaaron Mein ek Nayi Yojna*)

September 1933
Translator: Keerti Ramachandra

Even if at some later date films are of some benefit to us, and make education and health easier (to comprehend), the current trends in cinema cannot be said to be reassuring. If the progress of our society is solely dependent on young men and women shamelessly and brazenly hugging and kissing in public, on scenes of crime and violence, then we are undoubtedly treading a dark path towards the future. Europe's immorality with all its vices have taken firm root here, but Europe's industriousness, dynamism, and enterprise among several other virtues, which this wantonness effectively draws a curtain over, is nowhere to be seen. It is said that the blame lies with this primary industry, the ramifications of which are immeasurable. Perhaps it has prevented vast amounts of money that was paid to import foreign films, from leaving the country. But the unfortunate part is that this income lies in the hands of a few moneybags, who without compunction, are leading the people towards a world of social injustices. They are only concerned about their profit; the country can go to heaven or hell. I am certainly not against the cinema. However, I definitely oppose how it is being misused.

Undoubtedly, people need entertainment, but in a poverty-stricken country like ours, they need food much more. Entertainment does not mean whipping up our basest instincts. The right entertainment guides us towards noble good thoughts. That is why we were heartened to note that the Madras Film Censor Board has constituted a committee to examine what influence films have on the minds of young men. They have prepared a questionnaire and sent it to all parents, requesting them to fill it as they wish, and send it back along with any suggestions they may have. Some of the questions were:

Does watching films have any impact on the boys' studies? Should boys watch movies often or only sometimes? In what state of mind do the boys return home from the cinema hall? How do they refer to (the halls) at home? Do they recount the scenes and dialogues from the film? Do they praise any particular actor or actress? Do they only praise them or express a desire to emulate the life of the actor? Do young men and boys pick up positive or negative influences from films? Does cinema affect character-building lessons, exercise awareness of one's duty, sense of responsibility, in young people? Can cinema be assumed to cause moral corruption, which therefore presents a distorted view of life to the youth? Or encourages them to stray from the path of moral rectitude? Give examples to support your answer. What kind of films do you consider suitable for young men: historical, cultural, dramatic, comic, or educational? What kind of films do young men choose, according to their predilection?

We hope that the committee will consider all the views expressed in this matter and come to an agreement, the announcement of which we await with bated breath with the views expressed. We wait eagerly for the announcement.

26

Broadcasting in the Countryside (*Broadcasting Dehaaton Mein*)

September 1933
Translated by: Ruchi Nagpal

A gentleman has arrived from England to examine the kind of grounds which are suitable for broadcasting in India. All eyes are set on the countryside. Broadcasting should be publicized in every village and corner, and it should benefit millions. There is no doubt that broadcasting can significantly facilitate citizens. It is the only medium that can connect them to the larger world. Speeches of great learned personalities, music from across the world can be made accessible to the people in the countryside within minutes. However, it is not a charitable organization that will design its programmes for the sole benefit of the people. It will also aim at generating maximum profits for itself, and in the age where everything is causing harm instead of benefit, there will be definite exploitation of this as well.

27

Ramleela in Prayag
(*Prayag Mein Ram Leela*)

September 1933
Translator: Ruchi Nagpal

We are delighted to know that after 13 years, the Ramlila festival will be celebrated in Prayag without any hindrance. The Collector of the district of Prayag has ssuggested the ideal of an egalitarian society by accepting that every community has the right to celebrate their religious festivals.

28

An Appropriate Advice
(*Ek Uchit Paramarsh*)

September 1933
Translator: Ruchi Nagpal

In yesterday's edition of the *Leader*,[1] a gentleman has requested the head of education, Mr. Mackenzie, that in every school, half a day on Saturdays should be officially separated from the curriculum for extracurricular activities. Debate, drama, scouting, first aid, etc. subjects are not given as much importance by the school officials as should be. Since the responsibility of the teachers is limited to the qualification of boys in examinations, teachers, rightly enough, look at these subjects as futile because it does not affect their performance in examinations. The education department also thinks that these subjects should be taught to the boys but leaves the final decision with the headmasters. The result of it, being dependent on the headmasters is such, that, sometimes these subjects are paid attention but

1. *Leader* (October 24, 1909-September 6, 1967) was one of the most influential English-language newspapers in India during the British Raj. Founded by Madan Mohan Malaviya, the paper was published in Allahabad. Under C.Y. Chintamani, a dynamic editor from 1909 to 1934, it acquired a large readership in North India. Apart from Premchand's work, many of Mahatma Gandhi's writings were also published in it, and it is the repository of important writing of that generation.

the moment the headmaster starts following the old school, then these subjects are not touched upon. If the head of the education department will issue a notice that the schools must dedicate one day a week for these subjects, then this question will not remain subjective anymore. There is no need to mention that the importance of these subjects in the psychological development of the students is no less than mathematics and geography. It is slightly higher than these subjects in certain aspects. However, there is a definite hurdle that, as of now, it is rather challenging to find competent teachers for these subjects, and therefore the responsibility is given to the teachers who do not know these subjects well. It is the primary reason for their despondency. We only work with dedication when we have adequate knowledge and experience of the subject matter. If there is no excitement in the teachers, then why would students be inclined towards that subject? If some attention is indeed paid to the subjects, then it is done for the sake of it, and therefore it does not interest the students. The education department has not yet paid attention to these issues. If the education department will consider these aspects in their inspection and include it among other responsibilities of the teachers; and also fix a time for it, then surely such useful learning will not be neglected.

29

New Ideals of Education (*Shiksha ka Naya Aadarsh*)

September 1933
Translator: Sami Rafiq

The ideals of education in the world so far have been merely to satisfy social needs. Till date, individualism has been supreme in society, and our education system too has focused on the individual. One's progress starts from childhood and is completed in university education. Being shaped in such a mould, a young man becomes self-serving, excessively selfish, making friends out of self-interest and an opportunist, and a snob. Our education system does not awaken our social consciousness; instead, it aims to use society for one's own ends. Society exists only to provide opportunities for one's progress and accumulation. Those people alone are considered successful who can exploit society to the fullest. The system is such that an individual is compelled to walk in that direction because there is no other way.

However, a revolution is taking place rapidly in our society. Whether communism spreads or not, the ideals of society have changed. Countries like India may be steeped in worries for heaven for another ten or twenty years, but the world is moving towards collectivism, and in truth, the essence of collectivism is that it brings equal opportunities to each individual, does not bestow rights based on birth or belief and is close to godliness. What is individualism, but the exact opposite of this?

The global brotherhood is the highest ideal of human civilization and religion. It has been our goal since the earliest times, but perhaps we have never believed in the loftiness of such an ideal, or we have thought it the last step in the ladder of religion and thus unattainable, which has placed us as far from it as we were a thousand years ago. But even today, there has never been a higher ideal, and even today, the soul of the world is looking towards that timeless future with hopeful eyes. Intellectuals are gradually coming to the unanimous opinion that in order to obtain this ideal, we would have to create the world again; in other words, a society in which competition is replaced by supportiveness, in which people start trusting each other instead of doubting each other. Moreover, they may not gain the power to oppress others; rather, it should be to help others. The education system in today's world breeds jealousy, fear, repulsion, greed, selfishness, and cowardice, and this process starts from the stage of childhood. Parents who are well off are excessively indulgent towards their child, and when he grows up, their attempts to make him better than others results in making him useless and his thinking is transformed in such a way that he becomes nothing more than a blood-sucking parasite of society. In this respect, our gurukuls were better than the Etons or Harrows or Princes' Colleges of today in which all students were equal. Such a system created a feeling of commonality in them. Now even intellectuals in the West can see that the education system that they have embraced for centuries creates a weak character and strengthens anti-social traits that sow the seeds of disharmony and separateness. The existence of imperialism, professionalism, and the conflict between nations are the results of this defective education, which by focusing on the importance of the individual, makes him a violent animal of society.

The biggest revolution in the field of education is the understanding that at the age of five or six, the adult personality is laid down. The moral character that is developed at this time cannot be changed later. So far, we have not given much importance to childhood, and because of our ignorance of this stage, we have managed to spoil the future of children altogether. It is at this age because of our ignorance, that children start to lie, make false excuses, and also learn to steal. It is at this age that the habit of laziness and the opposition towards the principles for a healthy life are formed. It is at this age that they become stubborn, selfish, and cowardly. In this regard, the parents have a greater responsibility than before for the moral character of their child. Some experts believe that the child learns good and bad habits in the very first year of his life. Since the child cannot be sent to school at this age, it becomes the moral duty of the parents that before becoming parents, they should thoroughly familiarize themselves with the principles of good parenting. It is now accepted that children possess more or less the same traits and the use or misuse of those traits make them good or bad.

30

Press in India
(*Bharat Mein Press*)

October 1933
Translator: Madiha Musarrat

While addressing the condition of newspapers in India, Sir C.V. Raman rightly said that the editing of newspapers is like walking on a stretched rope and an editor has to be always alert. Otherwise if the balance is disturbed, the editor can fall into the pit of "Press Act" or can even be on the verge of defamation. He rightly articulated that in such occupations, there is a sword hanging ominously all the time. Economic difficulties make the condition even worse. The only reason for this is that people here do not want to pay for reading a newspaper. While travelling in a train when a gentleman purchases a newspaper, all the exciting gazes are fixed at the paper, and people shamelessly begin asking for it. We experience this every day. The question here is not that of poverty. Nobody expects it from the labourers and the starving farmers that they will read a newspaper. However, even when educated people who can spend 5-10 paisa daily on cigarettes and betel nuts also borrow it from others to fulfil their desire, in such a situation, how can newspapers survive? So the question is as to how newspapers can create an impact on the people of our country as they do in other countries. How will newspapers impact our country the way they do in other countries?

Most of the papers survive on advertisements, and they keep their avenues open for the publication of all kinds of advertisements. The editors blacken page after page on the boycott of foreign products, but they glorify them through their advertisements. However, they are helpless. If they do not do that, their newspaper will not last a day. In other countries, thousands of educated youth while working in newspapers attain name and fame. There is no scope here.

31

The Ramlila of Prayag Shut
(*Prayag Mein Ramlila Bandh*)

October 1933
Translator: Madiha Musarrat

In the last issue, we expressed happiness that after nine years this year, the Ramlila is being organized, and Hakim District had given permission for the procession of the parade. However, when Mr. Bishop gave the order, the police commissioner of Prayag was in Nainital. When later he returned, he immediately notified all the four Ramlila committees that the parades have to get back to the Ramlila Maidan before evening. Although it is not stated clearly, the meaning of the notification was to inform the parades to take place before the Muslim evening prayer; otherwise, he will not be able to take responsibility for any violation of peace. Ramlila committees did not accept the agreement, and the Ramlila had to be adjourned. We cannot say that the police commissioner of Prayag consulted the Muslims of the city before coming to this conclusion, or he had thoughts about the communal clashes. According to our knowledge, the Muslims did not have any objections. We can also agree that, even if some Muslims might have issues with it, why should a community festival be stopped because of them? What is the government for? Isn't it their job to ensure each part of the society gets help for their legitimate work? Why will the government evade this responsibility?

32

The Tours of Justice Young
(*Justice Young key Daure*)

October 1933
Translator: Madiha Musarrat

Justice Young, owing to his fearless judiciousness, has won the respect and love of the whole nation within a few days. It is a matter of great pleasure that he is continuing the scope of his area of service. While touring many districts, he is benefiting the scout movement. However, Sewa Samiti scout should be merged with Baden Powell scout or why not Baden Powell Scout to be merged with Sewa Samiti, this is incomprehensible. Sewa Samiti is a national organization; it is as national as it can be in the present circumstances. Baden Powell is a foreign organization whose soul is also foreign. When both institutions are similar, then it would only be appropriate to break the Baden Powell Scout and merge it with Sewa Samiti. If Justice Young does not do this, we would advise him to keep his services limited to the high court where his services are well-appreciated.

33

Annihilation of God in Hindi Literature (*Hindi Sahitya ke Ishwar ki Chheechhaledar*)

November 13, 1933
Translator: Keerti Ramachandra

In a November issue of *Saraswati* magazine[1], Shri Pandit Venkatesh Narayana[2] Tiwari wrote a highly considerate and thought-provoking article drawing the attention of readers and Hindi litterateurs alike, towards the genre of writing that has come to be known as 'Bhaktiras,[3]' devotional literature, in which love has been portrayed in its basest, most raw and vulgar form. The poets of Brajbhasha[4] have spent their entire lifetime writing about the secret dalliances and heartfelt yearnings of Kanha[5] (Krishna), Radha and the *gopis*. Certainly, but if the Hindu religion is condemned for this and Christianity and Islam are projected as free from these emotions, it is a grave injustice perpetrated on the

1. The first Hindi monthly magazine of India. Founded in 1900, by Chintamani Ghosh, the proprietor of Indian Press, in Allahabad.
2. A Congress Member of Parliament from, Kanpur District (North) in the first Lok Sabha.
3. Intense love and devotion towards God. Some poets add it to the classical nine rasas.
4. One of the two predominant literary languages of North-Central India (the other is Awadhi) before the switch to Khariboli in the nineteenth century.
5. A diminutive form of Krishna.

entire Hindu community. Sufi poets have written poems of the love between Prophet Muhammad and Allah, in which references are made to the Prophet's tresses, his beautiful shapely eyes, and his sugar candy speech. In Christianity, even today, there are daughters of Mariam who devote their lives to the service of Christ. Do you know a certain Nawab of Awadh was an ardent follower of the *Sakhi dharma?* He used to be cloistered in his home for three days every month and not meet or interact with anyone. Even today, one sees some *Muslim fakirs* belonging to this sect, wearing nose rings, earrings, thick bracelets, and anklets, with colourful *odhnis*[1] draped around them wandering about the *bazaars*. The Muslim community shows these *Sakhi* sect[2] followers great service and respect. The Hindu writers and poets have not said anything new; on the contrary, this is one instance of the human tendency to see God in human form. When you see God in the form of Krishna, how is it possible for the entire humanity to view God in the same form? After all, each one will perceive God according to our emotions, our preferences, and our predilections. Some might see him as Shiva, some as Ram, others as Krishna, or even as Vishnu. Those in whom the sense of dharma, righteousness dominates, sees God as Ram, those who consider loving the primary emotion will worship God as Krishna. Those in whom gratification of the five senses predominates, they become panchamakari[3]

1. A length of cloth used by women to cover the upper body.
2. One which has only male members who dress themselves as women (gopis to be specific) in order to reinforce their identity as sakhis or girlfriends of Krishna and to attain the esteemed spiritual emotion known as *sakhi-bhava*.
3. One who practises the "five observances," "five Ms" or "five essentials" five substances used within a Tantric practice: they are madya (alcohol), māṃsa (flesh), matsya (fish), mudrā (ring), maithuna (sex).

or Vamamargis[1] and worship at the *Bhairavi chakra*[2]or the feet of the goddess Bhairavi. Ram, Krishna, and Shakti are all manifestations of our diverse emotional perceptions of God. It is impossible to safeguard idol worship from these evils. It is this practice of giving a concrete form (to deities) that is the root of all improper conduct. Because of its great influence, lakhs of people become devotees of Lord Shiva and get intoxicated on opium and cannabis. However, others offer sacrifices at the altar of the Devi, while many more dance and sing in the presence of Krishna. Once you accept god in a concrete human form, it is not possible to keep him pure and unblemished, free from human weaknesses. If you desire wealth, how can God not help you acquire it? Enormous temples are built in his name, where he resides, festivals to celebrate his birth, marriage, and other rites are held, thieves burgle after seeking his blessings, usurious moneylenders swallow huge sums at interest rates and grow their bellies; in God's name land holdings are purchased, trade commerce takes place, cases are filed and fought, whereas the long-suffering poor and downtrodden surrender themselves to him and forget their troubles. However, this is not the feature of the Hindu faith alone. Christians, Muslims and Buddhists, are all victims of this disease. In fact, the *Muslims*[3] believe in a formless god, and in Buddhism, there is no mention of a god. Once you have accepted God in a human image, you cannot help but attribute human pragmatism to him. As a result, he will eat

1. A member of the tantric cult which prescribes flesh, wine and women as essential to worship.
2. Another name of Durga. She is the creator in the muladhara *chakra* in the form of Kamarupa, which consists of three dots forming an inverted triangle, from which all triads are born, which ultimately leads to the creation of this universe.
3. Muslim. This is how members of the community are referred to in Hindi/Indian languages.

and sleep and he will seek pleasure, give birth to offspring, smile with joy, weep in sorrow, if the occasion demands he will lie, even be deceitful, but because he is a godly human being, all his human misdemeanours will be coloured by divinity making them omnipotent and omnipresent. If you are content with a half or quarter *ser*, should God not expect at least a *mand* or two? If you can win over a couple or more people, will he not conquer a countless army? Just because a few marriages are enough for you, should he deny himself the pleasures of two thousand women? If so, then your concept of God itself is flawed. It can be said that the creation of such a god has given birth to all these ills.

Come to think of it, where is the difference today between sin and virtue, wickedness and righteousness, aesthetic and obscene, sacred and profane? When eminent scholars advocate sex education, when the institution of marriage is being touted as unnatural for human beings, and we are told that what we consider evil and sinful is the result of social injustice, that these things are inevitable in the way society is structured today, so why keep harping on good and evil? Literature cannot be removed from life, so why do we expect poets to immerse themselves in search of truth and spirituality? If we can wash away our sins by taking a dip in the Ganga, why shouldn't the poets sing verses in praise of this holiest of holy rivers? Whatever a poet writes, he writes for people, so when he is a product of the same value system, how can you expect him to rise above it?

But no, the Hindi poet today is transcending those sentiments. He has no interest in Shyam's dalliance with the *gopis*[1] or his butter-stealing escapade. He does not sing

1. The maidens who were Radha's companions and shared her devotion/love for Krishna.

paeans to the *Ganga,* nor does he compose verses in honour of the celestial beauties, the *apsaras*[1] or the gods of love. He does not adorn his poetry with descriptions of the beauty of an oblique glance, or the stealthy theft of a heart, the sweet song of the anklets or the titillation of erotic situations. His themes are the human heart and its feelings, and he is a worshipper of the beauty of nature. There is no place for a lover's kiss, a devotee's devotion, and delight; he is not anchored in the concrete, but one with the rhythm of the infinite and the eternal. For him, the petal of a flower, the blush of dawn, the twitter of birds, the tears of an orphan, a maiden's nubile and beauteous form, the humble dwelling of a poor farmer, or a traveller wandering along on his journey—they are all equally attractive, novel and beautiful. He views the entire earth as a storehouse of beauty, he finds sources of joy scattered along his path, and he gets intoxicated by sipping a single dewdrop off a leaf. He brings to literature a new message, a new life, a host of feelings, where passion does not intrude, but only the poet's pure love and genuine yearning shines through. He is taking society towards purity and humanity because he has freed himself from the clutches of the man-god.

1. A celestial maiden of divine beauty.

34

Carmichael Library's Diamond Jubilee (*Carmichael Library ki Heerak Jayanti*)

November 20, 1933
Translator: Ruchi Nagpal

Carmichael Library[1] was established in 1872. In this way, it has been 60 years since its institution. Preparations are going on for the celebration of its diamond jubilee. Honourable Mr. J.P. Srivastav, the education minister of the United Province, has agreed to be the chief guest for the occasion. It is not only one of the oldest but also one of the largest libraries of the province. The late Rai Shankara Prasad, along with the help of some prominent citizens of the province, laid the foundation of this library. The library progressed with the

1. The Carmichael Library at Bansfatak in Banaras is one of the oldest libraries in North India. It was founded in the year 1872 by Sankatha Prasad Khatri, the then Commissioner of Banares. It was named after Carmichael. C.P. Carmichael was the elder police officer of the then Northwestern Province (which later became Uttar Pradesh) and was also the Inspector General in the Northwestern Province. Carmichael had a keen interest in art, literature and Indian culture. C.P. Carmichael became interested in the promotion and development of this library. Owing to his efforts, the Municipality of Banaras in 1875–76 gave an amount of Rs. 1,000 to the Library for construction in the Chowk area. During the national movement, this library also became a centre for witnessing the activities of the national movement and the people involved in it.

joint efforts of the citizens and government officials. Earlier, this library was located near *thathari bazaar* chowk, down the road that led to the park. The present chamber of the library was built at the back, and in 1876, it was opened for the public. The exposition of yesteryears gives us some information about the present condition of the library. The main hall of the library, which is 92 feet long and 21 feet wide, had a total of 126 newspapers/magazines for the readers, out of which 23 were daily news journals and 43 monthly. There were a total of 17,567 books out of which 7,513 were English, 3,595 Hindi, 2,883 Urdu, 2,383 Sanskrit, 939 Bengali, 138 Gujarati, and 76 Marathi. The library had 218 members. Income was Rs. 10,572, and the expenditure was Rs. 11,807. This description highlights the significance of this library. A former executive of the Banaras Municipality, Officer Rai Bahadur Jagannath's father, was the librarian in the initial years. In his memory, Mehtaji is spending Rs. 2,000 on building a room for the library. It is hoped that the votaries of education will take more interest in the matters of the library and will help to improve the administration so that more people can be benefited. People can only benefit from the library if it has a good collection of books along with a well-drafted catalogue of all the books. It must also be ensured that the maximum number of people should benefit from the library. A library that has an ample collection of old and new books and also has a significant number of readers is the most extensive.

35

Cinema and Youth
(*Cinema aur Yuvak*)

December 1933
Translator: Shuby Abidi

The kind of scenes that are primarily shown in movies and the adverse effect that they have on the character of the youth has led many countries in Europe to impose a legal ban on young people less than 16 years of age to see films. Scenes of murder and dacoity are shown so vividly that they do not have a positive effect on anyone. It has such a harmful impact on the young hearts that they try to enact it in real life, and they have landed in prisons. Nevertheless it can be hoped that educational movies can be of great benefit. The teaching of various subjects like geography, history, medicine, etc. has become very easy and exciting because of movies. The experts of educational theories find weaknesses even in educational movies. Their influence is not so bad as to lead people towards crime, but they do obstruct intellectual progress. There is no way to satisfy the curiosity of the boys. They only see with their eyes, but they do not get any opportunity to use their intelligence and sense of discrimination. This way, they become pleasure–loving; their faculty of reasoning becomes weak. They even admit that their mental weakness has grown to such an extent that they do not recall the fine details of it. Children's practical sense and their tendency to discover new things are entirely suppressed. The vogue of cinema is growing every day, but it is hard to find a decent film. Till this profession goes into the hands of educated, enlightened, and people of character, there is no hope of its improvement.

36

Convocation Speech of Sir P.C. Rai
(*Sir P.C. Rai ka Deekshant Bhashan*)

December 18, 1933
Translator: Ruchi Nagpal

In the convocation speech of Kashi University, Sir P.C. Rai raised some critical questions which need to be considered. For instance, according to him, lectures should not be made mandatory in the universities, and instead, students should develop a desire to learn themselves. Schools destroy the imagination of the students by stifling them with the syllabus. There is no doubt that the examinations and lectures limit the self-development of students, and therefore we have so many great men who never saw the face of a school even once. However, in my opinion, why do we consider BA students as University students at all? What is known as secondary education in our country ends with matriculation, and by that time, students are only 15 or 18 years of age, and their reckoning power had not developed. In reality, that reasoning power gets developed till the BA. Beyond this, three years should be dedicated to the university in which lectures should not be made obligatory, but the students should be able to assess and research on their own. Education till the BA should be economical and made available to as many students as possible. Nevertheless, it is rather astonishing that in these times of recession when the incomes have dropped school expense has drastically increased. The bureaucratic authority, which is ruling the other sectors, has upheld its authority over schools as well. The same long salary bills, same examination fees, and the same air to terrorize the students. An ordinary school teacher is no less than a police officer or a deputy magistrate when it comes to establishing authority. Well, it is a controversial topic, and there will be many who will second it or stand against it, but perhaps nobody will have any objection against the ideal of education through the mother tongue, which you have set forth. In Hyderabad, students have been attaining higher education in Urdu. What can be said through Urdu can be said through other languages as well, but the problem is that every state has its different language. Even the number of main languages would not be less than a dozen. If the state language becomes the medium of education in every state, then we can not envisage the impact it will have on the idea of nationhood. Our students will forever remain limited in their vision. Therefore, it is vital to adopt the national language as the medium of education and not the mother tongue. Moreover, it has been decided that no language other than Hindi is capable of becoming the national language. If Bengal accepts this offer, then we are hopeful that other states will also accept it. If the national language becomes the medium of education, then it will be possible to finish the intermediate course in matriculation with ease. And then there is hope that students will not become arrogant as they do after having read English, which makes them incapable of business and agricultural practices. However, the need for a Western language will always remain. There is no sustenance without it. We need it to keep pace with global developments.

37

Speech by Sir Tej Bahadur Sapru
(*Sir Tej Bahadur Sapru ka Bhashan*)

December 1933
Translator: Ruchi Nagpal

In his convocation speech at Allahabad University,[1] Tej Bahadur urged for a change in the curriculum, which can solve the question of livelihood for students because the question of livelihood is much higher than the question of civilization. You have often said that the youngsters are idling in the streets with their science, law and art degrees without any gain. You paid more attention to professional education. May I ask, is there a place for industrial students anywhere? Let us not talk about the technical schools of Roorkee and elsewhere; there are not a large number of opportunities for carpenters, blacksmiths, and other menial workers. If their number increases, there will be unemployment in their community as well. Which profession, then, will solve the question of unemployment?

1. Sir Tej Bahadur Sapru, KCSI, PC (December 8, 1875-January 20, 1949) was a prominent Indian freedom fighter, lawyer and politician. Tej Bahadur Sapru was born in Aligarh in the United Provinces (now Uttar Pradesh) in a Kashmiri Hindu family. Sapru worked in the Allahabad High Court as a lawyer where Purushottam Das Tandon, a future nationalist leader, worked as his junior. He later served as a Dean of the Banaras Hindu University.

However, it is not just a question of livelihood. It is a question of honour and a luxurious lifestyle. Are youngsters forbidden to have aspirations like other people? Nobody has ever seen a carpenter or a cobbler residing in a bungalow. The maximum he could ever do is to buy his wife jewels or reconstruct his house. The people who are living an honourable life are the ones who have degrees in law, science and engineering. The youth of our nation is following the same path. They cannot be satisfied with the notion that they are born to tie shoelaces, and higher education will be harmful to them. Whatever they see around impacts them in a very significant way. Those who teach them, those whom they idolize, those who enrich their intellect, how can they possibly have no impact on them? When such people preach professional education to him, he is envious and thinks that they are living a beautiful luxurious life and are advising him to indulge in a hard life. This is the reason why, despite being utterly hopeless, they still rush towards schools. There is still some hope for the top two students but nothing for the rest. What if luck favours him and he becomes one of the two? Whatever may come, he will not give that up soon. He will try his luck a few times, and if he then fails, he will have the comfort in knowing that he did try with his complete will. His young spirit will never be prepared to run away from the field and see himself as incapable.

The way society is organized, it was inevitable for such a situation to arise, and it did. As long as some people will use their intellect to achieve their ulterior motives, it will give way to other such people also to use their degrees as a passport and reside in the world of honour and luxury and the students in schools will remain in such a wretched condition even when schools become a mere graveyard of their aspirations. This condition is not only prevalent in India. All the developed countries, including America and Europe, where man reigns supreme, are suffering from this condition. If the nation does not become unified, if a handful of clever people continue to reap monetary benefits, if the people will not give up their selfish ways and the nation will not realize its responsibility that every individual has the right to live and prosper equally then the unemployment of the educated youth will prevail in the same manner. It is true that many big countries are governed by people who have never been to school. However, people like Maloney, Hitler, and Stalin have not reached their goals by following the conventional societal path. They reached their positions through revolution, and revolution is not a child's play. We cannot let this idea foster in our youth that the doors for success are closed on them, and they can only revolt against the system to find a place for themselves. It will be a sad day for our nation if this idea is fostered in the hearts of our youth. Thus, it is necessary that the nation must recognize this principle that diplomas and degrees are not the gateways to power and property. Only then, the real importance of education will be realized. Education has become a profession where one can obtain degrees by spending money, provided one should not be completely witless. For the prospective progress of the nation, the present condition of the society and nation, wherein a handful of people who have monopolized the resources and are spreading the feeling of struggle and discontent, must be changed. Luxury and pride should not be the criterion of our greatness but our sacrificial nature and service towards the nation.

38

Doctor Tagore in Mumbai (*Doctor Tagore Mumbai Mein*)

January 1934
Translator: Ruchi Nagpal

It is an art to extract donations from the public, and there are two such artists in India. One is the noble Malaviyaji[1], and the other is Mahatma Gandhi. It is rather difficult to say who is superior of the two. The two stalwarts must be placed in the same category. Malaviyaji collected lakhs of rupees when the economy was booming. In these days of the recession, Mahatmaji has collected 2.5-3 lakh rupees from just two provinces. We have heard, Malaviyaji is also getting ready for the same. These two leaders have become veterans in this art form as they have been practising it for the past 50 years. Doctor Rabindranath Tagore is a world-renowned poet and a great artist, but when it comes to the art of begging, he needs to learn from these two beggars. He has recently arrived in this area. Malaviyaji raises money through his magical oration and high praise of the tradition, whereas Mahatmaji collects the money and scolds people

1. Mahamana Pandit Madan Mohan Malaviya (December 25, 1861—November 12, 1946) was an Indian educationist and politician notable for his role in the Indian independence movement. Malaviya strived to promote modern education among Indians and eventually founded Banaras Hindu University (BHU) at Varanasi in 1916, which was created under the BHU Act, 1915.

as well. It is his unique quality. Doctor Tagore organized a paid event where he had the students of Shantiniketan perform. He also participated in the event, but it is heard that they could not raise a reasonable sum. The point is, if people are not enthusiastic about the institution for which the funds are required, then it becomes rather tricky to raise funds. Shanitiniketan is yet to find a place in the hearts of the people. Unless they place a record of their services and sacrifice before the people, they may get funds from a few wealthy donors, but it will be challenging to get any funds from the public. However, we could not find the noble doctor Tagore as daring as he is believed to be. If Shantiniketan can produce any students who can attest extraordinarily in the battle of life, then the nation will shower the same love to Shantiniketan as it has accorded to gurukuls.

39

Sectarianism and Culture
(*Saampradayikta aur Sanskriti*)

January 15, 1934
Translator: Ameena Kazi Ansari

Sectarianism always appeals to culture. Perhaps embarrassed to reveal its true self, it dons the attire of culture just like the ass donning the skin of a lion to intimidate the animals of the jungle. Both Hindus and Muslims aspire to preserve their culture until Judgement Day. Each believes that their culture is pristine, but they forget that now there is no such thing as 'pure' Muslim culture or Hindu culture, nor is there any other 'pure' culture. There now exists only one culture in the world and that is the culture of economics. However, until today, Hindus and Muslims continue to lament the fate of their respective cultures even though there is no connect between culture and religion. There is Aryan culture, there is Persian culture, there is Arab culture, but there is nothing like Christian culture or Muslim culture or Hindu culture. Hindus worship idols, but don't Muslims also pay obeisance at mausoleums or shrines? During Moharram, don't Muslims offer sherbet and sweets to processions carrying richly-decorated *tazias* or replicas of the tomb of the martyred grandson of Islam's Prophet? Don't they consider mosques to be the houses of God? If there is a Muslim sect that considers it heresy to pay obeisance and bow before the greatest of prophets, then there is a faction among Hindus which considers their gods to be just pieces of stone, rivers to be just flowing currents of water, and scriptures to be just gossip. In these matters, I see no difference between their two 'cultures'.

So, do the differences have to do with language? Muslims might claim Urdu to be their language, but for Muslims in Madras (now renamed Chennai), Urdu is as unfamiliar as Sanskrit is for the Hindus of Madras. Whichever province Hindus or Muslims reside in, they speak the common man's local tongue, whether it is Urdu or Hindi, Bengali, or Marathi. The Bengali Muslim and Bengali Hindu cannot comprehend or speak Urdu. Both speak just one language—Bengali. The Hindus in the Frontier Provinces (in Pakistan after 1947) speak Pashto just like the Muslims there.

Then, can distinctions be made based on attire? If people from the Frontier Provinces are made to stand before you, you would find no difference in what they wear. Hindu men and women there wear the same kind of *salwar* as Muslims; Hindu and Muslim women dress in the same kind of *kurtas* and similar *odhnis*. Hindu men also don the same kind of caps and turbans. They even have beards that look similar to those of Muslims. Go to Bengal, and you see both Hindu and Muslim women wearing *saris*; Hindu and Muslim men there wear the same *kurtas* and dhotis. The trend of the *tehmat*, wrapped around the waist, is a recent one, visible ever since sectarianism has gained ground.

Now let's take the case of cuisine. If Muslims eat meat, then eighty per cent of Hindus are also meat-eaters. Hindus of high social standing consume liquor as do Muslims of the same class; so do Hindus and Muslims from the lower classes. Middle class Hindus consume very little alcohol, or they prefer bhang pellets made from hemp. The true monarch of bhang is the priesthood. Middle class Muslims also drink very little; there are some, though, who enjoy the drowsiness of opium with their Hindu brethren. Yes, there are Muslims who sacrifice cows and consume their meat, but even among Hindus there are groups that consume cow meat even though there is not much difference between the meat of hunted animals and others that have died naturally. In the world, Hindus are the only ones that consider cow meat to be inedible, or eating it to be a sacrilege. So, should Hindus withdraw from the worldly dilemmas of faith?

Music and painting are also a part of the culture, and here, too, one does not find differences. One knows of the art of the Mughals, and, along with Hindus, they sing the same ragas and compositions. Muslims might not have had a tradition of drama, but in today's times, we find Muslims involved just as much as Hindus in acting.

Given all this, I am at a loss to understand which culture's protection evokes such intense sectarianism. In reality, the call of culture is mere pretence and sheer hypocrisy; its propagators are people who rest in and enjoy the cool shade of bigotry. Theirs is nothing but a strategy to draw simple gullible folks towards sectarianism. The guardians of Hindu and Muslim culture are those worthy individuals and groups who have neither faith in themselves nor in their fellow countrymen or even in truth. That is why they continuously believe in the necessity for power, which, like a village headman, is often a catalyst in fomenting discord. Those possessing such power hardly care for the joys and sorrows of the masses; they have no social or political agenda to place before the nation. Their only effort is to oppose others and then appeal to the government for redressal, thereby ensuring long-lasting foreign rule. To them, foreign rule is more acceptable than

Hindu or Muslim rule. They compete with one another for positions and favours, doing nothing more than being the ruler's assistants. If Muslims have been able to extract favours from the ruler, why should Hindus not do the same and, like the Muslims, enjoy the same benefits? Such is their psychology! To think of something which will unite Hindus and Muslims for the betterment of the nation is beyond their mental capacity. Most sectarian institutions comprise the wealthy middle class, the landowners, officers, and those hungry for status. Their area of operation is to seek opportunities for their own community so as to rule over them by exercising their economic and commercial clout. They do not care for the welfare of the common masses. Such institutions are instantly prepared to oppose those policies of the government, which, despite being beneficial for the public, are seen to be detrimental to institutional interests. On going deeper into the issue, we shall discover that in these institutions, most gentlemen have some vested interest. If nothing else, their access to the mansions of power is easier. The incredible thing is that bureaucrats look upon such men with great respect and treat them with immense regard. The only reason for this is that bureaucrats know their power flows from such men, irrespective of their personal squabbles that damage each other. Make them a request and observe their callousness, their invincibility. It is amazing to see that some of these people have furtively started spreading the rumour that Hindus on their own can obtain independence. They even quote from history in this regard. By circulating such misconceptions, they only add to Muslim disaffection and achieve nothing else. If there were times Hindus enjoyed freedom when Muslims held sway, then there were also times when Muslims established empires during Hindu rule. Just forget those phases of time. It will be a blessed day when history rises above such narrow confines of thought. This is not the time that sectarianism has reared its head. This is the age of economics, and the only policies that succeed will be ones that address economic problems. It is a time to erase blind faith and hypocrisy in the name of religion and a time to put a stop to the practice of milking the poor dry. Today allows neither time nor scope nor need to defend that culture, which is the vice of the wealthy, the greedy, and the callous. For the poor, survival is the primary concern. After all, what else is there in culture for them to defend? An ignorant public is invariably attracted to religion and culture. As awareness dawns, people become aware that it is merely the swindler's culture to defraud them in the guise of either a ruler or a scholar or a businessman. The public today is more concerned about protecting its livelihood, which is far more critical than safeguarding its culture. For ordinary people, an outdated culture holds no attraction. Sectarianism has only made them close their eyes to their economic woes, and tread a path that ensures their weak dependence for a very long time to come.

40

The Way of the Wind
(*Hawa ka Rukh*)

January 29, 1934
Translator: Ruchi Nagpal

A reporter of a newspaper in England has written that twenty-five years ago in Cambridge, literature, and poetry were the only topics that engaged students. Politics interested no one. The same Cambridge is ringing with the calls of communism today. However, the people have forgotten that twenty-five years ago nobody had even heard of the word communism. When science made nuclear weapons, how could there be no turmoil in the political arena? What could attract the youth in the parties of generous and highly traditional people? Those who oppose communism are the ones who wish to dominate others and get a better share of everything. Those who envisage an egalitarian society and do not assume a unique position will never oppose communism. Youth are idealistic. Take India, for example; fathers are worshippers of capitalism and sons oppose it. The youth can see that the current socio-political system crushes their high idealism and sacred feelings and turns them into selfish, heartless beings. Why should they not then turn against such a system which is killing their humanity and substituting their empathy for a hard ending struggle? In the words of the same reporter, "It will be hard to find a rational man who will not accept the communist solution to the present condition."

41

Prohibition on Dance in Germany (*Germany Mein Naach par Bandish*)

February 12, 1934
Translator: Ruchi Nagpal

Hitler's government has forbidden youngsters below the age of 18 to attend a strip dance performance. They might go if accompanied by an experienced person. Passionate and self-indulgent youth folk of Germany have opposed this rule, but the German government does not care for such protests. There is an increased inclination of people in Europe towards such activities. The hypocrisy of the situation is that the people who shout slogans for women's safety and respect are the ones to seek voyeuristic pleasure by looking at nude girls. I want to appeal to those youngsters to welcome this order rather than opposing it and spend their time in some manly activities instead of wasting it on strip dance.

42

Swami Satyadev School (*Swami Satyadev Paathshala*)

February 19, 1934
Translator: Ruchi Nagpal

Readers will be delighted to know that the famous Hindi writer and national volunteer Swami Satyadevji, who is a wandering ascetic, has made Kashi the centre of his work field and will reside here. He will continue to serve the language through his works and has now also established a school. Kashi is the best place for a school like this because the place has always been a centre for education. This school will impart education in the subjects which will make a child diligent, a free thinker, generous, intellectual, and independent. Swamiji has seen the world and has thoughtfully studied the rise and fall of empires. He is not a worshipper of false asceticism, which looks at life as transient and this world as the root cause of all the sorrows and miseries. He has sensitively compared all the religions of the world. Therefore, it can be envisaged, the kind of education which will be bequeathed by him. History of Europe, emergence and development of Western thought and philosophy, cultural developments in the east as well as in the west will be taught in great detail. This school will be one of its kinds in Kashi, where there will be a confluence of western and eastern thoughts. One cannot say whether an institute like this will get success in a place as orthodox as Kashi, but one cannot help but agree that Kashi being traditional and ancient has always welcomed new ideas, and we can only hope that Swami Satyadevji will be successful in his promising endeavour.

43

The Spirit of Indian Art
(*Bharatiya Kala ki Aatma*)

February 26, 1934
Translator: Poonam Sharma

At the annual exhibition of the Lucknow School of Arts, His Excellency Sir Malcolm Talley conferred a beautiful deliberation of Indian art. He suggested that the ancient Indian art has always been an expression of some religious, mythological, and philosophical ideas which are distinctively Indian. In his view, this is the soul of Indian ethnic art. Certainly! However, in that age of fanaticism, which ethnic art form in the world could be devoid of this kind of aesthetics? When the entire world yielded to these artistic traditions, how could India be any different? Just as the Buddhist artists invested their talents in portraying the life of Gautam Buddha and the great Italian painters and sculptors indulged in the depiction of Jesus and other religious interests, Indian artists too invariably imbued their work with the stories of Lord Krishna's *Rasa Lila* and other mythological figures. The soul of India is the soul of the Indian artist, and for the contemporary times, it has freed itself from the religious and communal bonds of expression and is prepared to embark on a journey of self-independence. He alone will be the real national artist of present-day India who will be able to render this spirit in his art. The representations of Indian gods and goddesses, as well as the Indian monarchs, have become only a subject of admiration, and the national sentiments of contemporary India no more derive inspiration from them. However, there are still those intellectuals who rejoice in the funny stories of Lord Krishna and compose volumes in their veneration. However, they are only those complacent and latent people who have neither bothered to engage with the reality of contemporary times nor will their indulging circumstances spare them the will to do so.

44

A Sigh of Relief for the Editors
(*Patrakaaron ke Liye Santosh ki Baat*)

April 30, 1934
Translator: Ruchi Nagpal

The condition of journalists in India is not hidden from anyone. There would hardly be anyone who would strive more than this with the small allowance they get. Many of them do not even get a subsistence amount. They sell their property, if any; otherwise, they give tuitions to sustain themselves and publish journals. Those who get some foreign advertisements or legal notices from the court after much persuasion can have a decent meal at the end of the day, but those who are not that fortunate are mere living corpses. What grave injustice that they fill columns after columns with the cry of 'swaraj' but earn their bread and butter by publishing the advertisements of foreigners. They have no time to listen to the sweet blabber of their children. They are busy analysing and criticizing the assembly speeches of Sir Hailey, Sir Haig, or Sir Matron. One may ask if the Indian labourers of South Africa are debarred from the land then why are you jumping out of your trousers? Nobody else is commenting. Lawyers are debating the issues with content. Merchants are converting their money into gold with great pleasure, and landlords are contently receiving large amounts from their tenants, and our journalist is shedding tears of blood after some unfortunate labourers. Hitler, Mussolini, Churchill and Roosevelt said something, and our journalist here loses all sense. If a robbery happens, they feel as if the robbers took their arms and parts away, if the police fires a shot, they feel as if they have been shot. If this is not madness, then what is it? How will a madman become mad? In my opinion, journal publication is sheer madness, craziness, and obsession.

45

Riots during Festivals (*Tyohaaron Mein Dange*)

April 1934
Translator: Ameena Kazi Ansari

The situation in our land has deteriorated to such an extent that no festival goes by without rioting or violence in some half a dozen places, and some people losing their lives. Whether it is Moharram or Eid, Holi, or Dussehra, riots do occur. When these festivals come around, joy is replaced by worry and fear. If these occasions pass peacefully, we heave a sigh of relief. Things have come to such a pass that the issue of rioting during festivals no longer surprises us; rather, we are surprised when they do not occur on these occasions. So, riots keep happening. They happen on issues so ridiculous that they evoke laughter. It is almost as if spirits possess people. Sometimes there is a clash because a Muslim boy's faith is stained by droplets from the *pichkari*, or water gun, of a Hindu boy. At other times, it could be about the particular route to be taken by Moharram processionists carrying a decorated *tazia* or over which tazia will lead other *tazias*. It is on such issues that *lathis* and knives are drawn, and the blood of innocents is shed for a bogus defence of faith. Thus is the brotherhood of generations throttled, and the seeds of enmity sown for the future. Ironically, it is on festive occasions that educated people emerge to show their muscle. They might never have said *namaz* even once in their lives, nor ever visited a *mandir*, or ever shown any sympathy for their fellow beings, but they join issue for snatching the fame of martyrdom on festive occasions. It would be better to put a stop to all festivals. Festivals come around for people to celebrate happiness for a day or two, to forget their daily worries, and to affectionately interact with each other. Here in our land, there is bloodshed during festivals. Till as long as untouchability, discrimination, and hypocrisy in matters of faith prevail, there is no opportunity for the situation to be remedied.

46

Guru Tradition in India (*Bharat Me Guru Pratha*)

October 1934
Translator: Shuby Abidi

Guru Pratha is available in different names in the whole world, but it has made India its hub. The Vice-Chancellor of Lucknow University Dr. Paranjape recently gave a very enlightening lecture on this topic. While comparing blind faith and intelligence, he observed that in ancient Hindu scriptures, the stature of a teacher had been stated with such intensity that a teacher is given more importance than God. In many places, this path has caught up so much that when a newly married daughter-in-law arrives, she is offered first to the guru. How the guru blesses her, no one knows except the woman, or if they even know, then it is not considered to be his lewdness but his favour. It is not necessary that a guru has to be sacrificial. Many teachers live in great luxury, but if the guru is self-denying and has repudiated social norms and ethical behaviour and wanders around in a small strip of underwear, then his magic works very fast. This guru doesn't let wealth approach him, doesn't even touch money, just rejects it. Moreover, they are showered with wealth. They may accept it with both hands, but yes, they maintain the façade of renunciation as if they accept the gifts for their students' sake and that they are averse to money. This guru immediately creates a new course in which the disciples will go straight to heaven and will be free from transmigration, which is the main objective of an Indian. For this new path, a new kind of sectarian mark and a new way of worshipping is thought about, and the ideals of which are so high that it is reduced to nothing but a mere pretence. In this path, everything becomes praiseworthy, which in a healthy state is disdainful. At times the rights of saints increase so much that the disciples have to contribute a share of their income regularly. One cannot criticize any work of the saint. Furthermore, it is hilarious that there are not just fools in this group; great scholars keep aside their intelligence, discard their ideas and perform the secret rituals with complete blind faith, and they believe that others are deprived of the pleasure that their soul is enjoying. Several times their secrets have been revealed; nearly every day, a saint is exposed, but it has no effect on the public, and they are always eager to welcome a new saint. Saints talk in riddles, which can be interpreted in various ways. If their prediction proves right, nothing like it. Their miraculous powers become very popular. If it turns out to be incorrect, then even that is accepted as truth. The saint must have some uniqueness. If they sustain themselves by consuming milk or bananas or ash, then you can consider them to be God. In many places, you get Pauhari baba, who lives just on air. Those saints who speak English and are fun-loving can go to America and earn both money and popularity. We do not know if the existence of such saints will ever stop or not.

47

Health and Education
(*Swaasth aur Shiksha*)

March 1935
Translator: Ruchi Nagpal

Our education system is not free from blemishes, but according to me, its most significant defect is its saddening attitude towards health. For a man to live in the world, it is not essential to know geometry, history, and other ludicrous subjects, but it is relatively vital to know how to stay healthy. The result is such that they become very knowledgeable mentally, but their physical health takes a back seat. Most of our educated men are walking ailments. Some suffer from indigestion, some from heart disease. Also, diabetes has become so pervasive that there is no questioning it. The reason is that during our childhood, we were not taught the importance of health, and we were not encouraged to look after our health. So when one realizes the importance of health and vigour as a youngster or as an adult, then it equates to watering a haystack. Now eat as much as you want or binge on all kinds of vitamins, but sound health will still evade you. During our childhood, a book titled *Ways of Good Health* was taught to us during middle school, which had short lessons on air, water, light, etc. Even today, there are lessons on health in our primary readers, but these lessons are taught to the students like they are taught grammar and history. In fact, these subjects are taught more forcibly because if a student fails any of these, then the students eventually fail. Lessons on health are taught from the mere perspective of language, and the primary purpose of these lessons is not touched upon. The terror of examinations is such that students have no time to breathe. Also, then there is our attitude which does not stir a revolution regarding this issue. Our son must earn an MA degree even if he loses his eyesight or suffers severely through indigestion. This is our mentality.

It is a widespread belief that for good health, it is essential to have milk, meat, nuts, butter, etc. in our diet. Most of our youngsters become so desperate and hopeless with financial problems that they take no interest in physical exercises and yoga, whatsoever. What is the benefit of exercise when they cannot get nourishing meals? Exercise will benefit if they get almonds and milk in the morning and proper proteins through meat, eggs, etc. However, they are unaware that science has established that our ordinary meal of vegetables and wheat has the equal nutritious capacity as milk, eggs, and nuts for a healthy body, provided we take the diet correctly. If unknowingly, we discard the beneficial parts of our products, then it is our fault and not of the product. It makes us happy to see that science is directing us in the same direction in which we were heading all along. With education and aping of Western culture, we have sidelined the use of things which make our diet healthy and wholesome, and pursue items which are bought to us through Western advertisers— Ovaltine, Quaker oats, malted milk, etc. as if all the nourishment lies in these things only. All the youngsters are after these things, but now it has been proven that the nourishment which is there in our raw and leafy vegetables like carrots, spinach, and radishes cannot be found in these highly promised products. Money and succumbing to our desires make us go astray. We will not consume jaggery, which is full of nourishment. We need sugar, as clean as possible. A myth has been circulated that jaggery is unsuitable for health. We also do not consume new rice. The older the rice, the more satisfied we feel. It should be as blooming as a flower. We forget that the older the rice gets, the less nutritious it becomes. We have similar myths with wheat as well. We enjoy eating refined flour, which is very finely ground. It is outrageous and an example of illiterate behaviour to eat wholesome wheat, and it is beyond our comprehension to digest choker. It is not even fit to eat. However, now, science has indeed proven that choker is the most beneficial part of wheat. *Neem* twigs have won over toothbrushes and toothpaste, but this myth still convinces us that it keeps our teeth healthy.

However, the most prominent harm is done from the ignorance we have towards the natural functioning of our senses. During adolescence, when our senses get developed, many youngsters ignorantly abuse them to deplete their bodies and health. They seem to be unaware of the fact that they are indeed uprooting their life through such ostentatious desires. All our senses have a specific function to perform. If we use our mouth instead of hand and hand instead of the foot then it will be challenging to live. However, the pity is that nobody tries to enlighten us on these issues, which are in complete darkness. If an expert on these issues is asked to deliver a talk in schools and colleges, then it will put a halt to the misconduct which takes place in secrecy. There is a need for an expert in biology to write a good book for students, which should guide them about the need for a chaste and healthy body. It should tell them that they are indeed harming themselves out of ignorance. It would have been beneficial if parents could educate their children regarding such issues, but the orthodox web which entangles our society is hard to be broken off, and many people cannot break off this false qualm. The books on sexual education published in our country are not written from that perspective; publishers have not produced them for social welfare but rather to earn money. Moreover, such books never dictate a righteous path to children, but they rather titillate their senses and imagination. This is not a work by poets and writers but rather by doctors and celibates. Some scholars in Europe, on the other hand, have started exploiting this critical, serious issue and are promoting certain ideologies that are fraudulent and digressive. Therefore, there is a greater need to bring out verified literature on this issue. Along with this, it is imperative for schools that they should not look at the intellectual development of the students as the sole fulfilment of their duties but should also view it as their responsibility to develop their health, psyche and worldview as well for their holistic development.

48

Birth Anniversary of Mahatma Gandhi (*Mahatma ji ki Jayanti*)

October 1935
Translator: Ruchi Nagpal

We are highly privileged that we have arrived at that happy moment in national history when the entire nation will celebrate the birth anniversary of Mahatma Gandhi. We also pay our homage in greeting. The kind of awakening which Mahatmaji's character has kindled to the nation can be called revolutionary, and the high ideal of life which he has put forth has raised humanity way above divinity, which is the supreme imagination of our ideal humanity. Moreover, what else is literature, if not the throbbing of our hearts? If we read carefully, then we will be able to mark out a clear difference in the literature before and after the day of Gandhi. The literature which the Gandhian age has produced is vibrant with activism, fearlessness, ideas of simple living and high thinking, and the desire to sacrifice life for one's principles and values. It has put a restriction on the fatuous discussion of 'Art for art's sake,'[1] which was

1. 'Art for art's sake' is the English translation of the French slogan "L'art pour l'art" which is credited to Théophile Gautier (–1811 1872), who was the first to adopt the phrase as a slogan in the preface to his 1835 book, *Mademoiselle de Maupin*. It expresses a philosophy that the intrinsic value of art, and the only "true" art, is divorced from any didactic, moral, politic, or utilitarian function.

going on and is still prevalent, which looks at the use of literature as grotesque. By emphasizing the use of art and literature, Mahatmaji has extracted it from the trough of susceptibility. According to us, beauty is the sole validation of an object. Had it not been useful, it had not been beautiful and thus not truthful at the least. By elevating the status of Hindi to the national language, Mahatmaji has given a rare example of political foresightedness, which only he is capable of. The dream of a national literature which the nation is envisaging today is a result of Mahatmaji's doing. The kind of unprecedented glory which the language has attained because of his assiduity and diligence is unsurpassable. By giving this nation a national language, you have indeed given voice to the mute, and if we choose to walk on the path set forth by you, then the day is not far when there will be an amalgamation of national, literary and cultural ethos of Hindustan.

Such works are sometimes described as "autotelic", from the Greek autoteles, "complete in itself", a concept that has been expanded to embrace "inner-directed" or "self-motivated" human beings.

49

Literary Developments of Prayag Women's University (*Prayag Mahila Vidyapeeth ki Sahityik Pragati*)

February 1936
Translator: Ruchi Nagpal

The progress of Prayag Women's University since its inception is commendable. The university has purchased its own land and has started working towards the construction of the building. The annual expenditure of the University is Rs. 32,000, and due to the laudable economic management of the founder, a significant share of this expenditure is met by the fees given by the students. The University does not have to request the government or the municipality for any funds. Further expenditure is met by donations. The monthly fee is only 8 rupees, which is used, not only to provide education, food, accommodation, etc. to the students, but it is also used to provide for the students who are incapable of paying the fees. Such an arrangement makes us admire the economic skills of Mr. Sangam Lal. This University has pursued the ideal of providing the best education to students for the minimum fee. It prepares the girls for vernacular exams in just three years. It has also arranged for dance, music, exercise, and other co-curricular activities within the University. We are delighted to see that girls from states like Assam and Madras are also getting educated here. What makes us even happier is the fact that girls come out of this University as independent, self-sufficient beings who can succeed in all walks of life. Since the time Mahadevi Verma has taken charge of the administration of the University, it has been progressing speedily. Literature has also entered the busy domains of the University. The first women's storytelling competition in Hindi was also held at Prayag University on the 26th of January. Honourable Shirvani Devi presided over the event. Stories by women are often published in magazines and newspapers, and the women read several unique stories in this event, out of which Kamla Choudhary and Kamla Devi Sharma's stories were the best. Kamla Sharma's creation was autobiographical, each word of which was imbued in sheer brilliance. Tragic, serious stories are not much liked at such confluences. Light-hearted, good-humoured stories are appreciated by the audience on such occasions along with the art of delivery, which should be mastered by the storyteller. In the next issue, we will discuss the speech delivered by the chairperson.

50

New Policies of Prayag Women's University (*Prayag Mahila Vidyapeeth ki Nayi Yojanaayein*)

April 1936

Translated by: Ruchi Nagpal

Last month we published an application of Prayag Women's[1] University. We hope that kindhearted men must have paid due attention to it. It is disheartening to know that an Institute which is trying to solve the problem of women's and girls' education in the face of opposing situations is dependent on money. For various reasons, English medium schools and colleges are not proving beneficial for our girls. Moreover, if there are some beneficial elements, then due to the high-cost ordinary people are unable to reap those benefits. It has instead become a luxury. Prayag Women's University gives quality education to girls at minimum

1. Prayag Mahila Vidyapeeth is a Women's College based in Allahabad. It was founded by Mr. Sangamlal Agarwal, an enlightened citizen of Allahabad with the aim of providing education to women, who appointed Mahadevi Verma as its first Principal. This Vidyapeeth is located in a locality called Dakshin Malaka in Allahabad. Through this institution, private examinations 'Praveshika', 'Vidya Vinodini', 'Vidushi' and 'Saraswati' were taught. Sangamlal wanted to spread education among women through these examinations.

cost and helps in an all-round holistic development of girls, which makes them efficient with household chores as well. This year, the University has come up with a scheme, which will help mid-qualified girls to pass their entrance exams in three years and otherwise trained and skilled girls to pass the examination in two years. It has been the University's motto to give maximum knowledge to girls in minimum time, and these two schemes aim at the same. It takes the girls a minimum of five years to qualify for their entrance examination after they have cleared the middle or higher-level exams. An institute, which substitutes five years with two, is definitely making the lives of these girls easy. The monthly fee for this University is only Rs. 15, which includes tuition fees, hostel charges, food, etc. As of now, the University has provided only 15 girls with this arrangement. Those parents who are interested in benefiting from this opportunity may write a letter to the registrar and can reserve a seat for their daughters.